THE SECOND AND THIRD EPISTLES
OF ST. PAUL TO THE CORINTHIANS

THE SECOND AND THIRD EPISTLES OF ST. PAUL TO THE CORINTHIANS

WITH SOME PROOFS OF THEIR
INDEPENDENCE AND MUTUAL RELATION

BY

JAMES HOUGHTON KENNEDY, D.D.

ASSISTANT LECTURER IN DIVINITY IN THE UNIVERSITY OF DUBLIN
EDITOR OF "S. HIPPOLYTUS ON DANIEL"
AUTHOR OF "NATURAL THEOLOGY AND MODERN THOUGHT," BEING
THE DONNELLAN LECTURES, DELIVERED BEFORE
THE UNIVERSITY OF DUBLIN, 1888-9

WIPF & STOCK · Eugene, Oregon

Wipf and Stock Publishers
199 W 8th Ave, Suite 3
Eugene, OR 97401

The Second and Third Epistles of St. Paul to the Corinthians
With Some Proofs of Their Independence and Mutual Relation
By Kennedy, James Houghton, D.D.
ISBN 13: 978-1-5326-0149-1
Publication date 7/15/2016
Previously published by Methuen & Co., 1990

CONTENTS

PART I.
THE DATE OF FIRST CORINTHIANS . . . PAGE 1

PART II.
THE IDENTIFICATION 79

PART III.
GREEK TEXT OF SECOND AND THIRD CORINTHIANS . 163

PART IV.
ENGLISH TEXT OF SECOND AND THIRD CORINTHIANS 184

PREFACE

IN the first part of this volume I have laid before the reader reasons which appear to me to show that the Epistle which is known to us as 1 Corinthians was not written (as is generally supposed) in the spring of the same year in which St. Paul left Ephesus, but about a year earlier; and that, consequently, it cannot be the Epistle of whose reception by the Corinthian Church St. Paul first received news from Titus after he had come into Macedonia. The second part gives the proofs which have led me to the conclusion that the Epistle with which 1 Corinthians has for so long a time been wrongly identified has not been totally lost, but that a considerable portion of it has been preserved for us, and is to be found in the last four chapters of the document which appears in our Canon as 2 Corinthians. The concluding portion of this volume will enable the reader to see and examine for himself the result of this theory exhibited in a concrete form.

The former of these conclusions is not unfamiliar to modern Biblical critics; though, I think, some of the arguments which I have employed in support of it have never been published before. Many leading theologians in England, as well as in Germany, have publicly avowed their belief that the attempt to identify 1 Corinthians with the Epistle described in 2 Corinthians ii. must be abandoned. The thesis, however, of the latter part of this book is (at least in this country) so novel that it must, almost of necessity, at the outset awaken the hostility of many readers. I shall certainly not complain of this, if it leads my critics to examine closely and rigorously the proofs which I have laid before them. I believe that the theory which I advocate has nothing to fear, but everything to hope, from the result of able and honest criticism. I only ask that it may not be condemned unheard.

The question at issue is not one in the examination of which criticism seems foredoomed to failure for want of material. The personal character of St. Paul's Epistles to the Corinthians, and the frequent references to current events which they contain, ought to supply critics with abundant material for testing a theory which not only substitutes two Epistles for one, and interposes between them an interval of some months and the visit of Titus to Corinth, but also reverses the order in which the chapters have hitherto been placed. If the traditional order of the text be the true order, it is scarcely possible that so violent a disturbance of

PREFACE

it should not throw its allusions to recent history into hopeless confusion and chaos.

This is a test which, in the following pages, I have endeavoured to apply to the theory in dispute, and it will be found that, instead of causing confusion, it again and again enables us to discover order and coherence in what eminent critics have described as "a trackless forest"; nor does it substitute any fresh difficulties in the place of those which it removes. This line of argument is not to be confused with that which calls attention to the sudden and violent difference of tone between chapters i.-ix. and x.-xiii. There is no conceivable explanation of the fact that the same order of the text which confronts us with this unexplained and perplexing change of tone should also throw the historical references into confusion, except the explanation that both difficulties have been caused by the displacement of the original order.

There are, indeed, many independent lines of proof which establish the same conclusion, so that we must not only examine them one by one, but also take account of their cumulative force. The proofs, however, on which I lay most stress are derived from three passages in the Epistle which I have designated as 3 Corinthians, and which are all found in a paragraph in which St. Paul is avowedly speaking of the missing Epistle; in each of these passages he refers back to a corresponding passage in 2 Corinthians; and in each of the three pairs of parallel passages the act or purpose which in 2 Corinthians is present or future, in 3 Corinthians is spoken of as belonging to the past.*

It was not, indeed, any of these lines of proof which, more than a century ago, led Semler to suggest that the canonical Epistle contained matter which did not originally belong to it. He appears to have regarded the contrast between the parts as sufficient evidence for his theory, and to have sought for no further proof. He complicated his theory by advocating further alterations of the text, some of which he afterwards abandoned or modified. In fact, he divided 2 Corinthians into three epistles: (1) 2 Corinthians i.–viii., to which he added Romans xvi. and 2 Corinthians xiii. 11 to end; (2) 2 Corinthians x. 1 to xiii. 11; (3) 2 Corinthians ix. Meyer, in his reply to this theory, endorsed the statement of Hug, that we might as well divide the $\pi\epsilon\rho\grave{\iota}\ \sigma\tau\epsilon\phi\acute{a}\nu o\upsilon$ of Demosthenes into two orations because the first part is calm and the second part vehement. Semler's theory did not for a long time gain much acceptance even in Germany, and in England it was completely ignored; so much was this the case that Dean Alford, in his *Introduction to 2 Corinthians*, acknowledged

---

* The examination of these pairs of parallel passages will be found in the chapter which is entitled "The Identification."

that he derived his information about the theory solely from Meyer's reply to it. In process of time, however, fresh advocates appeared in Germany; and in the year 1870 Professor Hausrath, of the University of Heidelberg, published a pamphlet, entitled *Der Vier-Capitel-Brief des Paulus an die Corinther*, in which he advocated the division of 2 Corinthians into two separate Epistles, the division being made at the end of the ninth chapter. Hausrath went into more detailed proof of his theory than Semler had done; he particularised four points of difference which had arisen between St. Paul and the Corinthian Church: (1) The case of the incestuous person; (2) Suspicions about the collection for Jerusalem; (3) The announcement of St. Paul's approaching visit to Corinth and the subsequent postponement of the visit; (4) The controversy with the Judaising party there. Taking these points one by one he claimed that he could show that chapters x.-xiii. of 2 Corinthians represent an earlier stage of the controversy than chapters i.-ix. The treatise is marked by acuteness and ability, but in discussing each of the four heads Professor Hausrath frames hypotheses about the position of things at Corinth, and the accusations brought against the Apostle, which do not appear to me capable of being sufficiently established to become the foundations of an important theory; and by far the most telling part of the reply which was made by Professor Klöpper to the theory is, in my opinion, his examination of some of these hypotheses.

Since 1870 the question has become to some extent an open one in Germany, but in an article on the subject which I published in the *Expositor* in September, 1897, I was obliged to admit that in England it had as yet received very slight notice. Commentators, when they do not ignore it altogether, generally confine themselves to a passing reference to Klöpper's refutation of Hausrath's treatise.

A sentence in a short introduction to an unfinished Commentary by Bishop Lightfoot, which has been published since his death, appears to me to suggest that that great scholar regarded the matter as one which should not be dismissed in so summary a manner; for he classes both Hausrath's and Klöpper's treatises among works which "will well repay examination," while at the same time he refrains from expressing any opinion on the theory, or even stating it. This reserved attitude, taken in connection with his respectful mention of both the opponents, makes it probable that he suspended his judgment on the matter, and that, had time and strength been spared to him, he would have further investigated a subject which his words implied to be one that would repay investigation.

It was not by any of these writers that my own attention was first called to the question, but by a remark which was made in my hearing by the late

Dr. Reichel, Bishop of Meath, to the effect that he was convinced that there were two Epistles in 2 Corinthians, and that the one which was written last had been placed before the earlier one. His illness and lamented death, which occurred a short time afterwards, deprived me of the opportunity of further conversation on the subject; and, though I had a very high respect for his acuteness of mind and profound scholarship, I was at first strongly prejudiced against what appeared to me to be a mutilation of the Epistle. As I examined the text, however, proofs of various kinds appeared to multiply, all converging to the same conclusion — that the Epistle referred to in 2 Corinthians ii. 4 as written ἐκ πολλῆς θλίψεως καὶ συνοχῆς καρδίας was not our 1 Corinthians, but an Epistle whose closing portion we possess in chapters x.–xiii. of 2 Corinthians.

When I first came to this conclusion I was unaware that it had advocates in Germany, and I felt so strongly the difficulty of obtaining a hearing for it that I had no thought of publishing anything on the subject. It occurred to me, however, that if there were two separate Epistles, written by the same writer, with only a short interval between them, and referring to the same circumstances seen from such very different standpoints, it was not improbable that there might be some passages in which the Epistle which was written later would refer back either to the very phraseology of passages in the earlier Epistle or to the acts or purposes spoken of, or the thoughts or feelings which underlay the words of those passages. It was the discovery in this way of the pairs of parallel passages, of which I have already spoken, which first encouraged me to advocate in print the conclusions to which I had been led; and I eventually published articles on the subject in the September and October numbers of the *Expositor*, in the year 1897.

In the interval my attention had been called to Professor Hausrath's pamphlet by the mention of it in Bishop Lightfoot's *Notes on the Epistles of St. Paul;* for, though the bishop did not say anything about the nature of the work, the mere mention of the title—*Der Vier-Capitel-Brief*—appeared to me to suggest that the theory which it advocated might be identical with my own. When I procured the pamphlet I found that Professor Hausrath had not gone on the same lines that I had, and that even his conclusion was partly different from mine; for he believed that the four chapters were the whole of the Epistle written by St. Paul, and that they had probably been originally an appendix to an Epistle written by the brethren at Ephesus in support of him; while my belief is that we have in these four chapters only the concluding portion of an Epistle of which the earlier part has perished like the Epistle referred to in 1 Corinthians v. 9. I was, however, encouraged by finding that, though we had travelled by different roads, we had, in part at least, arrived at the same conclusion.

An article from the pen of Dr. A. Robertson, in the first volume of *Clark's Dictionary of the Bible*, which appeared in 1898, marks a new departure in the history of this controversy in England; for in this article Dr. Robertson fully recognises the importance of the question, and enters into a long and careful discussion of it. His conclusion is that "on the whole, as regards internal evidence, we may say that the case for separation is not proved; but it would be going too far to say that it is absolutely disproved."

The argument from internal evidence, on which Dr. Robertson appears chiefly to rely as partly disproving the case for the separation of the four chapters, has increased my sense of the importance of the difference between Professor Hausrath's theory and my own; for the validity or invalidity of this objection depends altogether on this difference. The objection is thus stated by Dr. Robertson: "The identification of these chapters with the painful letter would seem to demand that they should refer to the (*ex hypothesi*) still unsettled case of the Offender (chapters 2, 7). But no such reference can be traced; the argument for separating x.-xiii. from the rest of the Epistle thus loses a very strong positive factor."

This objection appears to me to tell with great

force against Hausrath's theory that we have in the four chapters an entire Epistle; but against the theory which recognises in them only the concluding portion of an Epistle of which the earlier part has been lost it has no weight whatever. If we had only the latter half of 1 Corinthians, we should have known nothing whatever about the incestuous person, for it contains no mention of his case. Our knowledge about him is derived from the fifth chapter, and from that alone.

In 2 Corinthians the case of the Offender would naturally be mentioned early in the Epistle. St. Paul tells us that he referred to this matter not for the sake of the man himself, but because of its bearing on the feeling of the Corinthians toward himself, and he would therefore naturally pass from the consideration of the offence to this question. I need scarcely add that chapters x.-xiii. are full of the latter subject.

A still later contribution to the literature of this question is to be found in an article in the *Encyclopædia Biblica*, by Professor Sanday, which also to some extent marks a new departure, both by what it omits and what it contains. It omits altogether the usual explanation that there was a rebellious minority, and that unfavourable news may have arrived after the ninth chapter had been finished. Not only are these points tacitly dropped, but, after giving a sketch of the received view of the Epistle, Professor Sanday adds, with that spirit of candour which inspires everything that he writes, "Considered quite broadly and generally, the course of events is clear enough; but when we attempt to give them precision in detail difficulties spring up at every step. The questions which arise are also exceedingly intricate, so that to state them satisfactorily is no easy matter. They have nearly all been brought to light by the research of the last five-and-twenty years."

Principal Robertson and Professor Sanday agree in the belief that the "Painful Letter" must be admitted to have been lost, and cannot be identified with 1 Corinthians. With regard to the painful visit, however, they differ. Dr. Robertson denies the visit; not indeed from the exegesis of the passages which appear to speak of it as having been paid, for he frankly admits that "the more obvious sense" of these passages favours it, but because he holds that "as a matter of fact the assumption of a visit ἐν λύπῃ does encounter hopeless obstacles, whether we seek to place it before or after 1 Corinthians."

Professor Sanday, on the other hand, rightly holds that the supposition that the second visit was only contemplated, not paid, is excluded by 2 Corinthians xiii. 2. He decides in favour of placing it before 1 Corinthians, and even possibly before the lost Epistle, which preceded 1 Corinthians.

This decision, in which he is supported by Schmiedel and other leading critics in Germany, involves the supposition of a duplication of the conflict between St. Paul and the Corinthians; for we learn from 1 Corinthians that St. Paul had only recently learned of the dissensions at Corinth, and of the moral offences there; and that he had learned them from report. This he repeats three times. If, therefore, the visit ἐν λύπῃ were paid before this Epistle was written, the causes of its painfulness must have been different; and indeed the absolute silence concerning it in 1 Corinthians is generally explained by the supposition that the matter had been so completely disposed of in the lost Epistle, which preceded our 1 Corinthians, that there was no need to refer to it further. Then (according to this system of chronology) came a new and more formidable revolt, and in consequence of this state of things the Apostle wrote the painful letter which was connected with the mission of Titus, and which is supposed to have been totally lost. Then, finally, after the second reconciliation, which resulted from Titus' mission, came our 2 Corinthians.

If this system of chronology were correct, is it conceivable that St. Paul, when at the close of this long series of events he wished to enforce a warning to those who were still rebellious, instead of connecting it with anything in his recent letter, or anything which he had said during the prevalence of the late rebellion, should pass over three letters and two reconciliations to revive the memory of words which

PREFACE

had been spoken in a controversy which to all appearance had been long dead and buried, and to connect his present warning with these words, as if nothing had happened in the meantime to change the situation, "I have warned, and I warn, as when I was present on my second visit, so also when I am absent now"? This appears to me to illustrate the manner in which the many allusions to current events in the Epistles to the Corinthians afford formidable tests for ingeniously constructed theories.

The eminent critics who have favoured this system of chronology were not ignorant that it involved great difficulties and improbabilities, but considered themselves coerced to adopt it by the same consideration which Dr. Robertson looked on as compelling him to deny the reality of the visit—*i.e.* the consideration of the purpose referred to in 2 (3) Corinthians i. 15, 16. Professor Sanday speaks of this point as having a direct and perhaps a crucial bearing on the question. His authority confirms me in the opinion of its importance, which before I saw his article had led me to describe 3 Corinthians i. 12-17 as a "Test Passage," and to devote to it three chapters (pp. 34-62). I believe that the true exegesis of this passage furnishes us with the key of the problem now before us.

I examined Professor Sanday's article with keen interest, to see what arguments so eminent, acute, and candid a scholar could bring against the theory on this subject which I believe to be true. I felt that if a strong case could be made against it, I was likely to meet with it now. Before concluding his article Dr. Sanday has brought forward three arguments in opposition to the theory in question.

The first is derived from 2 Corinthians x. 10: "His letters, say they, are weighty and powerful"; which Dr. Sanday looks on as a reference to the "Painful Letter." If this were so, it would, of course, be a complete refutation of my theory. But why should a description of St. Paul's letters, spoken of in the plural number, and in which no one Epistle is specially mentioned, be regarded as an identification? Why should not 1 Corinthians and the lost Epistle which preceded it be thus described? It cannot be objected that if it were weighty it could not have been lost; for, *ex hypothesi*, the "Painful Letter" must also be assumed to have been lost. There is no reason for the assumption that the first letter written by St. Paul to a church where he had laboured so long as he had done at Corinth, should be shorter or feebler than 1 Thessalonians; and that Epistle may, I think, very fairly be described as "weighty and powerful."

Professor Sanday's second objection is as follows: "When the Apostle wrote his painful letter, he wrote in order to avoid the necessity of making a visit in person (i. 23); but when he wrote these chapters he was on the point of paying a visit (xii. 14, xiii. 1)."

In the passage referred to above, *i.e.* i. 23, St. Paul is not stating the object for which he wrote, but giving the reason for his not having come again to Corinth: "To spare you I come no more to Corinth." For his statement of the object for which he wrote we must look a little lower down, *i.e.* in ii. 3: "And I wrote this same lest when I came I should have sorrow." His purpose, as it is here described by himself, was not so much to avoid paying the Corinthians a visit, as to prevent his visit when he paid it from being a painful one. This is the very purpose with which in xiii. 10 he avows that he is at that moment writing. "For this cause I write these things when I am absent, that when I am present I may not use sharpness." The statements prove more than similarity, they prove absolute identity of purpose; for "sorrow" ($\lambda\acute{\upsilon}\pi\eta\nu$) in ii. 3 is shown to mean the same with "sharpness" in xiii. 10, by the words which immediately follow: "For if I make you sorry" $\epsilon\grave{\iota}\ \gamma\grave{\alpha}\rho\ \grave{\epsilon}\gamma\grave{\omega}\ \lambda\upsilon\pi\hat{\omega}\ \acute{\upsilon}\mu\hat{\alpha}\varsigma$.[*] With this xii. 14 and xiii. 1 are not inconsistent; for they are warnings, and warnings are given to avoid the necessity of actual punishment.

The third objection is that there are too many

---

[*] This is one of the pairs of parallel passages which are discussed in the body of this work.

coincidences of expression connecting the four chapters with the preceding chapters to allow us to suppose them to belong to separate Epistles.

Professor Sanday gives a few samples of the use of these words, and rightly calls attention to $\theta\alpha\rho\rho\epsilon\hat{\iota}\nu$, as it is never found in any other Epistle of St. Paul, while it is used twice in the Four Chapters and twice in the Nine. But how is it used? In the Four Chapters, in one verse (x. 2) it is twice employed in a stern and painful way to express the Apostle's confidence against his opponents in Corinth; whereas, not only is this meaning of the word absent from the Nine Chapters, but the second time that it is used there the signification is totally reversed, and, instead of speaking of confidence "against them," he now writes: "I rejoice therefore that in everything I have confidence in you."

Another selected instance is $\pi\epsilon\pi o i\theta\eta\sigma\iota\varsigma$, which is used once in the Four Chapters, twice in the Nine, and only twice besides. This word, like $\theta\alpha\rho\rho\epsilon\hat{\iota}\nu$, is employed in the Four Chapters (x. 2) with the painful meaning of confidence against the rebels at Corinth. In the Nine Chapters, each time that it is used, it is used in a directly contrasted sense. In iii. 14, after saying affectionately that the Corinthian Church is his Epistle written in his heart, he immediately adds: "Such confidence ($\pi\epsilon\pi o i\theta\eta\sigma\iota\nu$) have through Christ toward God." In the only other passage in which it occurs in these chapters it again expresses confidence in the Corinthians (i. 15). This is the passage in which he speaks of his confidence that even in the past the Corinthians acknowledged him in part.*

Another word adduced is $ὑπακοή$, which is used in x. 5, where the Apostle speaks of the time when the obedience of the Corinthians shall be fulfilled, in a way which shows that he did not consider it as being fulfilled at the time when he was writing. In the Nine Chapters this word also is used in a directly contrary way, for there (vii. 15) the Apostle speaks of Titus as "remembering the obedience ($ὑπακοὴν$) of you all, how with fear and trembling ye received him." And he adds immediately: "I rejoice therefore that in everything I have confidence in you."

There are, no doubt, a great number of words which appear both in the Four Chapters and in the Nine; but a striking parallel to this is found in the verbal links between the Epistle to the Galatians and the Epistle to the Romans. In each of these cases the use of the same words and phrases seems to me to show that the Epistles which exhibit these points of resemblance were written about the same time, and when the mind of the writer was full of the same subject; but

* I have examined this passage at considerable length in the chapter which is entitled "A Test Passage."

not necessarily to prove that they must be parts of one and the same Epistle.

One of the foremost champions of the theory which regards 2 and 3 Corinthians as separate Epistles is Schmiedel, who in his *Hand-Commentar* has treated the subject with great learning and ability. I differ from him, however, on several points, in which he appears to me to have adopted hypotheses which, having been originally constructed to support the traditional account of the matter, naturally fit in badly with the truer view which he holds, and (that he may find a place for them) oblige him to multiply rebellions and reconciliations in a way which has been severely criticised by his opponents. Thus he holds that Titus was accused of over-reaching; and that he paid more than one visit to organise the collection. He also places the visit $\dot{\epsilon}\nu$ $\lambda\dot{\upsilon}\pi\eta$ before 1 Corinthians, and he believes that a promise to pay the Corinthians a double visit was made to them by St. Paul, and that its abandonment was made a charge against him.*

On the other hand, I hold that there is not the slightest proof of more than one rebellion or one reconciliation. That Titus had no commission about

---

* The body of this work was already in type before I observed a passage in page 79 of the *Hand-Commentar*, which anticipates my point about two of the pairs of parallel passages. It does not seem to have been noticed by any of Schmiedel's critics, as it is very short, and the idea is not developed.

the collection before the time of his last visit; and that he was never accused (so far as we know) of misappropriation of funds, but that his name is brought forward in 2 Corinthians xii. 18 because he was one of the last men whom the Corinthians would have dreamed of suspecting, and because (for that very reason) the mention of his name strengthened the force of St. Paul's argument and appeal. I hold that the reference in that passage is to an early visit to Corinth, in which he had followed up the missionary work which St. Paul had begun; so that he walked in the same spirit and in the same steps. It was, probably, because of the influence which he had thus acquired that he was afterwards chosen for the difficult mission which he so skilfully carried out; and his success in that mission induced St. Paul to send him back to promote the arrangements about the collection, which had probably suffered during the time of rebellion. With regard to St. Paul's wish to pay the Corinthians the double visit, I think that it was felt by him at some time between the visit $\dot{\epsilon}\nu$ $\lambda\acute{\upsilon}\pi\eta$ and the mission of Titus; but that it was only a wish, and never developed into a purpose, or was made the subject of any communication to them, till it was revealed to them in St. Paul's last letter in order to show that they had not been absent from his thoughts, and that he was not $\dot{\epsilon}\lambda\alpha\phi\rho\acute{o}s$, but had been earnest in his desire to come to them. Those commentators who regard it as impossible that the Apostle should have formed such a wish during the continuance of the rebellion, appear to have overlooked the fact that while the rebellion still lasted, Paul boasted to Titus about the Corinthians; thus showing that hope was all along mingled with his fear.

In connection with the question of the supposed improbability that mutilated manuscripts of two Epistles can have been joined together, Dr. Abbott has called my attention to the fact that the ninth and tenth Psalms are treated as one Psalm by the LXX., while in our present Hebrew text and English translation they are separate Psalms. We need not here debate which of these readings is to be preferred. In either case a mistake must have been made. Either two Psalms have been joined by some scribe, or one Psalm has been divided.* On the other hand, Psalm cxlvii. of the Hebrew text is divided into two by the LXX.

Professor Mahaffy has also reminded me of the Homeric Hymns to Apollo, which in the existing manuscripts appear as one poem, but which all critics agree in believing to have been originally separate hymns. He has also called my attention to the Egyptian Revenue Papyrus, in which

---

* See *Essays chiefly on the Original Texts of the Old and New Testaments*, by T. K. ABBOTT, B.D., LITT.D., Senior Fellow Trin. Coll., Dublin, Professor of Hebrew in the University of Dublin.

PREFACE

Mr. Grenfell has shown that the corrector desired to fasten on a supplementary roll containing the revised list of names, but that he made the mistake of allowing the same chapter to appear twice, immediately before, and immediately after, his new junction. The height of the papyrus, which here changes, is (Dr. Mahaffy remarks) clearly in favour of his hypothesis.*

In the prosecution of this enquiry my one aim has been the ascertainment of truth. At the same time, I am convinced that the tendency of the theory which I believe to be true, will be more conservative than is generally supposed. Dr. Robertson has remarked that "to this Epistle, more than to any other, we owe our knowledge to the true 'pectus Paulinum'—our intimacy with the Apostle's inmost self." Does not this give a new importance to the theory, if it be indeed true? Is it well that our impression of the Apostle should be falsified by our being led to suppose that the confusion and chaos which have been caused by the mistake of a copyist are a reflection of his inmost self?

My best thanks are due to the two scholars whom I have already mentioned, Rev. T. K. Abbott, Senior

---

* *The Revenue Papyrus*, edited by B. P. GRENFELL, M.A., Fellow of Queen's College, Oxford, Craven Fellow. With Introduction by J. P. MAHAFFY, D.D., Hon. D.C.L., Senior Fellow of Trinity College, Dublin, and Honorary Fellow of Queen's College, Oxford.

Fellow of Trinity College, Dublin, and Rev. J. P. Mahaffy, Senior Fellow of Trinity College, Dublin, for their valuable aid in the passage of this work through the press, and for the suggestions which they have made.

ST. PAUL'S SECOND AND THIRD EPISTLES TO THE CORINTHIANS

PART I.

THE DATE OF THE FIRST EPISTLE TO THE CORINTHIANS

THE DISPUTED JOURNEY AND THE DATE OF FIRST CORINTHIANS

THERE are three passages in the Second Epistle to the Corinthians (as it appears in our Bibles) in which there are apparent references to a visit paid by St. Paul to Corinth at some date intermediate between the time of his first visit to that city and the time when these passages were written. They are 2nd Cor. ii. 1, Ἔκρινα δὲ ἐμαυτῷ τοῦτο, τὸ μὴ πάλιν ἐν λύπῃ πρὸς ὑμας ἐλθεῖν: xii. 14, Ἰδού, τρίτον τοῦτο ἑτοίμως ἔχω ἐλθεῖν πρὸς ὑμᾶς: and xiii. 1, 2, Τρίτον τοῦτο ἔρχομαι πρὸς ὑμᾶς· ἐπὶ στόματος δύο μαρτύρων καὶ τριῶν σταθήσεται πᾶν ῥῆμα. Προείρηκα καὶ προλέγω, ὡς παρὼν τὸ δεύτερον, καὶ ἀπὼν νῦν, τοῖς προημαρτηκόσι, καὶ τοῖς λοιποῖς πᾶσιν, ὅτι ἐὰν ἔλθω εἰς τὸ πάλιν, οὐ φείσομαι. These passages have been dealt with by writers in two different ways. The earlier commentators, if they noticed them at all, endeavoured to show that the words used in 2nd Cor. xii. 14 and in 2nd Cor. xiii. 1, 2 did not necessarily imply that a second visit had actually been paid, but only that it had been purposed; 2nd Cor. ii. 1 had to be explained in a different manner, and was accordingly supposed by them to refer to St. Paul's first visit to Corinth. Later commentators on the other hand generally acknowledge that this mode of explaining the passages in question is unsatisfactory, and consequently admit that there was a visit paid to Corinth by St. Paul between the visits mentioned in Acts xvii. and Acts xx.; but they endeavour to show that the date of this second visit was earlier than that of the first Canonical Epistle to the Corinthians.

This method, however, of dealing with the question has not found favour with some even of the later commentators, who, in consequence of the difficulties which they have found in dating this second visit before 1st Corinthians, have fallen back on the more radical plan of denying its existence altogether.

Of these diverse methods of solution, that which denies the intermediate visit must be considered first; for it is clearly the logical course to examine the evidence for the reality of an event before attempting to determine its date.

The order in which the three passages above cited

THE DATE OF THE FIRST EPISTLE

were written is one of the points in which I differ from the traditional view. A reference to the text of the Epistles as they are printed in this Book will show that that which comes first in our Authorised Version is placed after the other two and is a separate Epistle. It would, however, be altogether premature to enter upon the discussion of this point at present. I shall, therefore, consider the passages without making any assumption about their chronological order; taking first that which is contained in 2nd Cor. xiii. 1, 2, because it is the longest and the fullest.

This is a passage whose importance and interest demand and repay a careful exegesis. Two ways of translating the second verse of Chapter xiii. have been suggested, and, if it is possible to determine which of these is the true rendering, it is possible also to determine whether the disputed visit was really paid or not. Those commentators who deny the journey render ὡς by "as if," making it introduce a fictitious supposition, and generally render καὶ by "though." This latter rendering indeed appears to be a necessary consequence of the meaning given by them to ὡς; for if καὶ were the simple copulative here, we must either regard both the suppositions which it connects (*i.e.* the presence and the absence) as fictitious, or regard them both as real.

The alternative translation renders ὡς by "as" and supposes οὕτως to be omitted before καί. This is the translation which is adopted in the text of the Revised

Version of the New Testament, "As when I was present the second time so now, being absent." The other rendering is given by the Revisers in the margin.

We have an instance of a similar omission of οὕτως before καί in Galatians i. 9—a passage which furnishes a most striking and suggestive parallel to this—ὡς προειρήκαμεν καὶ ἄρτι πάλιν λέγω.

If we confined our attention to the words ὡς and καί, either translation would be admissible. It is the context which must decide between them.

And first I would note the writer's introduction of the word νῦν. It appears from its position in the sentence to be intended to mark a contrast in time between the παρών and the ἀπών. The probability that he intended to mark such a time contrast becomes stronger when we extend our view to the previous clause "προείρηκα καὶ προλέγω," for in this clause we have an analogous difference in time between two verbs, which makes them appear to correspond respectively to the participles, προείρηκα to παρών, and προλέγω to ἀπὼν νῦν. Nor can it be objected that if this were the true connection of the passage, each participle should have been placed immediately after its verb; for the sentence gains in rhetorical force by the present arrangement which places the two warnings in juxtaposition. "I have warned and I warn as when I was present, so also when I am absent now."

The following clause—"τοῖς προημαρτηκόσι καὶ

THE DATE OF THE FIRST EPISTLE 5

τοῖς λοιποῖς πᾶσιν"—continues the parallelism, the προ of the προημαρτηκόσι marking the same difference of time between the pair contained in this clause, as has been shown to exist between each of the pairs in the previous clauses, and in the same order. We have thus three pairs in perfect correspondence.*

It will hardly be denied that the προείρηκα of xiii. 2 refers to a real occurrence, so that once the connection between the clauses of the paragraph is perceived, it becomes impossible any longer to regard the corresponding participle παρών as a fictitious supposition. But the question has further to be asked, "On what occasion did the Apostle previously make the announcement 'If I come again I will not spare'?" The supposition that this previous warning was given in a letter or through a messenger appears to be forbidden by the connection of the verb with ὡς παρών. In short the connection between these two clauses excludes two suppositions either of which would otherwise have been admissible. If the προείρηκα stood alone it might refer to an announcement made by letter. If the ὡς παρών stood alone it might be interpreted of a fictitious presence. But the conjunction of the two must refer to an announcement delivered during

---

* It may be noticed in passing that those who are spoken of as τοῖς προημαρτηκόσι would appear to be the same persons to whom St. Paul has just referred in xii. 21 as τῶν προημαρτηκότων καὶ μὴ μετανοησάντων.

a visit which was really paid by the Apostle to the Corinthian Church.

There are other considerations which strongly confirm this view, when we regard the passage in its entirety; for, if the journey in question is denied, the τρίτον of the first verse and the δεύτερον of the following verse refer to the same future visit; the δεύτερον being got by counting only real visits, the τρίτον by adding an intended visit. The latter mode of enumerating would indeed be somewhat peculiar. Number one is a visit; number two an intention which was never carried out, and this is number three. Such a mode of enumeration would have suggested the too obvious question — "Will then number three be like number one or like number two? Will it be an intention which will be carried out, or an intention which will not be carried out?" But once the reality of the disputed visit is acknowledged, the mode of enumerating becomes consistent and intelligible throughout the paragraph. The introduction of the word δεύτερον so soon after the mention of τρίτον, instead of causing confusion, as it would do if they both referred to the same approaching visit, becomes apposite and forcible. The whole paragraph represents an ordered progress to a foreannounced judicial act. The Apostle had warned the Corinthians when he was present with them on his second visit "If I come again I will not spare." He is now about to come again, and

THE DATE OF THE FIRST EPISTLE 7

on the eve of his third visit he reiterates the warning which he had given on his second.

I cannot find that any critic or commentator in England or Germany has ever attempted to suggest a possible object to account for the introduction of the supposition of a fictitious presence into the argument, or to give an intelligible reason why St. Paul should add to his warning the assurance that he gives it as if he were present the second time. The introduction of this supposition would not merely have been objectless, it would actually have destroyed the force of the warning which the Apostle was uttering with such emphasis; for it would have made him say that if he were already present on his coming visit he would utter by word of mouth the identical warning which he is sending to them by letter; whereas he is expressly telling them that when he visits them next he will do something altogether different—that he will then no longer threaten but perform.

The announcement of an approaching visit had already been made a little earlier in this Epistle (2nd Cor. xii. 14) and in connection with a like note of time; there as here it is spoken of as τρίτον. We have, however, in the earlier announcement a variation to which much importance is attached by those writers who deny an intermediate visit; for here he says not as in xiii. 1, τρίτον τοῦτο ἔρχομαι πρὸς ὑμᾶς, but ἰδού, τρίτον τοῦτο ἑτοίμως ἔχω ἐλθεῖν πρὸς ὑμᾶς: this addition is relied on as indicating that the true meaning of both passages is that this was the third time that he was ready, that he was prepared, that he intended to set out on his journey to Corinth.

The words ἑτοίμως ἔχω, however, do not of themselves determine the matter at all; for it is quite as admissible to connect the τρίτον τοῦτο with the ἐλθεῖν as with them; so that we may either translate the passage thus "Behold this is the third time that I am in readiness to come to you," or thus "Behold I am ready to come to you this third time."

The sentences which immediately follow may, I think, help us to see which of these renderings gives us the true meaning of the writer; for in them he informs his readers that during his coming visit he intends to live at his own charges and to make no demands upon their hospitality; and he reminds them that all his delegates to them have acted in the same way, so that this disinterested rule has been observed throughout. In this connection a reference to previous visits in which he had adopted the same independent course would be pertinent and appropriate; but visits which had not been paid in the body, but only in intention, could not possibly have made demands on the hospitality of the Corinthians; so that it would be difficult to discover what possible connection the mention of them could have with the Apostle's argument in this passage.

SECOND CORINTHIANS II. 2.

In this passage an overwhelming preponderance of manuscript authority connects πάλιν immediately with ἐν λύπῃ — τὸ μὴ πάλιν ἐν λύπῃ πρὸς ὑμᾶς ἐλθεῖν. The alteration in the order of the words which has been adopted by the Textus Receptus was probably (as Klöpper has remarked) caused by the assumption that St. Paul had only been once at Corinth.

Whether Klöpper be correct or not in his conjecture that the alteration of the text here was not purely accidental, but was caused by the copyist's belief that St. Paul had paid only one visit to Corinth before he wrote 2nd Corinthians, there can be little doubt that this belief has influenced the interpretation given to λύπῃ by some commentators, who have interpreted it as describing merely sorrow and depression of spirit which the Apostle no doubt often experienced during the visit which is recorded in the eighteenth chapter of the Acts. Indeed it would be difficult to fix on any epoch in his heroic career when he was long free from such experiences.*

The whole context however shows that λύπη has a very different meaning here; for the paragraph begins

---

* In this very Epistle he describes himself "as sorrowful yet always rejoicing."

with the solemn declaration contained in the twenty-third verse of the preceding Chapter "But I call God for a witness upon my soul that it was to spare you that I came not again unto Corinth"; and in the second verse of the second Chapter the writer shows that he is still pursuing the same train of thought; for the meaning which he intended to express by the word λύπη is clearly shown by the reason which he assigns for his determination not to visit them again in sorrow "*For if I make you sorry* who is he then that maketh me glad but he that is made sorry by me?"

These expressions show that the word λύπη refers to the severity which, but for the repentance of the Corinthians, the Apostle would have been compelled to exercise; and that it cannot be explained by any trials of his own such as those which he had to endure at the time of his first visit to Corinth.

The evidence for the intermediate visit which is furnished by these three passages is so strong that I believe it would long ago have been admitted by all commentators were it not for the difficulties encountered in reconciling it with the date which tradition had assigned to 1st Corinthians. The disinclination to admit its reality thus caused has, I think, been strengthened by the notion that if it had really taken place it must have been mentioned in the Acts. How little justification there is for this notion may be seen

<small>Objections to admitting the intermediate visit.</small>

from a passage in one of the very epistles with which we are dealing. In the eleventh chapter of 2nd Corinthians St. Paul tells us "Of the Jews five times received I forty stripes save one."

Not one of these occasions is mentioned in the Acts.

"Thrice was I beaten with rods."

Only one of these scourgings is recorded—that which took place at Philippi. And—most important of all in its bearing on our subject—we also read "Thrice I suffered shipwreck, a night and a day have I been in the deep."

Not one of these shipwrecks is mentioned in the Acts; for, of course, the shipwreck recorded in the 27th Chapter of Acts occurred long after the date of this Epistle.

If such thrilling incidents as shipwrecks have been passed over without the slightest notice, we have no right to feel any difficulty because the narrative omits to mention a voyage of a few days on a frequented route between two of the greatest sea-ports of the ancient world, where large vessels were constantly passing to and fro. St. Luke was not with St. Paul during the latter's stay at Ephesus, so that very little is told us of the events of those three years till we come to the riot which took place at their close. Not one of those plots of the Jews which Paul speaks of in his address to the elders of Ephesus is so much as mentioned in the direct narrative.

12 SECOND AND THIRD CORINTHIANS

But if this visit ἐν λύπῃ came between 1st and 2nd Corinthians, 1st Corinthians must have been written earlier than has hitherto been supposed, and a further consequence is that it cannot be the Epistle referred to in 2nd Corinthians ii. 4. Accordingly an attempt is now generally made to assign to the visit in question a date earlier than that of 1st Corinthians. We learn, however, from Galatians iv. 13, that when St. Paul had really visited a Church twice and had occasion afterwards to refer to one of those visits, he specified which of them he meant, speaking in that place of his visit as the earlier one, τὸ πρότερον, whereas in 1st Corinthians ii. 1 he refers to his original visit as if it were the only one he had paid them, κἀγώ ἐλθὼν πρὸς ὑμᾶς.

Can the visit be assigned a date earlier than 1st Corinthians?

Furthermore, throughout this Epistle everything is dated from this original visit. When St. Paul praises the Corinthians, he praises them because they remember him in all things, and hold fast the traditions even as he delivered them (1st Cor. xi. 2); and when he blames them, it is for their want of progress since his visit; "I fed you with milk, not with meat, for ye were not able to bear it; nay, not even now are ye able." An attempt has been made to explain away this by saying that the visit ἐν λύπῃ was so short that he here ignores it; but the change which a painful personal meeting between the Apostle and his converts (such as that visit plainly was) produced, could not be measured merely by the number of days that the visit lasted.

But a still stronger proof is furnished by the fact that in 1st Corinthians the Apostle in three several passages expressly says that he derives his information, both about their party spirit and their moral disorder, from hearsay evidence. "It hath been signified unto me concerning you, my Brethren, by them that are of the household of Chloe, that there are contentions among you." Again in Chapter v. 1 he writes, "It is actually reported that there is fornication among you"; and in xi. 18, "I hear that divisions exist among you, and I partly believe it." Is it conceivable that he could thus speak if he had previously paid them a visit in which these matters had been discussed between him and them, face to face, so that he spoke of it as a visit ἐν λύπῃ, and if he had then uttered such a threat as that to which he refers in 2nd Corinthians xiii. 2?

But if there is conclusive proof that St. Paul must have paid a visit to Corinth after he wrote our 1st Corinthians and before he wrote 2nd Corinthians (in which, as we have seen, it is three times referred to) it becomes necessary to abandon the attempt to identify 1st Corinthians with the Epistle which is described in 2nd Corinthians ii. 4, and in 2nd Corinthians vii. 8, for the whole context shows that from the day when that letter was despatched until Titus returned, St. Paul was in suspense and anxiety about the way in which it would be received: when he came to Troas after his departure from Ephesus he was still without news (2nd Cor. ii. 12, 13); and felt the strain which this absence of tidings caused him so keenly that he could not avail himself of the open door for the preaching of the gospel which he found at Troas, but pressed on eagerly into Macedonia to find Titus. In Macedonia the Apostle and his messenger met at last, and he plainly tells us that then and not till then did he receive the tidings for which he was so anxious.

Accordingly it has been tacitly recognised by all commentators that it would be hopeless to attempt to intercalate a personal visit of St. Paul to Corinth between the date of the letter referred to in 2nd Corinthians ii. 4 and the return of Titus. It is the recognition of the hopelessness of this solution, combined with the assumption that 1st Corinthians is the letter referred to in 2nd Corinthians ii. 4, which has forced some critics to explain away the journey by strained interpretations of the passages which speak of it, and has obliged others to place the visit before 1st Corinthians. The proper course in such a condition of things is to raise the question: Are we certain that the assumption which necessitates the strained interpretations is true?

THE DATE OF FIRST CORINTHIANS AND THE REFERENCES TO THE COLLECTION

This course ought to suggest itself even if we had no other evidence for the earlier date of 1st Corinthians than that which is connected with the question of the visit; but we have other and independent evidence of the strongest kind in favour of this earlier date. In 2nd Corinthians viii. 10, and also in 2nd Corinthians ix. 2, St. Paul refers to the Corinthian collection as having been ready a year ago; yet the directions given in 1st Corinthians xvi. make it plain that at that time the weekly collections had not begun, and the Apostle there gives directions about them as about a new thing. "But concerning the collection for the saints as I gave order to the Churches of Galatia, so also do ye. Upon the first day of the week let each one of you lay by him in store as he may be prospered, that no collections be made when I come." This system of weekly contributions was admirably suited to the circumstances of the Church of Corinth. Poor men, many of whom were probably weekly wage earners, and some of whom were perhaps slaves, could not give much at once; though out of their small earning they might put by a little every week. This would take time, so that two or three months at the least must elapse before they could be said to be ready. Even if we suppose that they commenced the system of weekly collections immediately on Titus's arrival, this would bring the date of their readiness very near midsummer. How then could the Apostle writing in the autumn of the same year say that he had been boasting of them that they were ready a year ago?

This note of time is, as we have seen, repeated twice by St. Paul (2nd Cor. viii. 10 and 2nd Cor. ix. 2), and if it is taken in its natural sense as describing the duration of the time which had elapsed since the Achæans could be pronounced ready, its evidence is decisive in favour of the earlier date for 1st Corinthians which is here advocated. An attempt has indeed been made to evade its force by maintaining that it does not necessarily imply anything more than the fact that New Year's Day had intervened between the time when the Corinthians were ready and the time when the Apostle boasted of their readiness, and that we might use a like expression in February when speaking of something that had taken place in the previous November or December, especially (it has been added) when as in these places the writer's intention is to make the most of the interval which has elapsed.

I think, on the contrary, that these would be the very circumstances under which we should have no right to do anything of the kind; and that if we did so, our hearers or readers would be disposed either to laugh at or to resent any serious attempt on our part to employ a purely arbitrary division of time like New Year's Day in order to make the most of an interval. This would be the case even now, when all the nations of western and central Europe have the same New Year's Day. In St. Paul's time there would have been still less temptation to adopt this device; for different men had different New Year's Days according as they used the Jewish, or one of the Greek, or the Roman Calendar. The last-named Calendar is never mentioned in this connection by those writers who adopt this line of argument, and I am not surprised at their avoidance of it; for the Roman Calendar puts New Year's Day on the 1st January, which would not suit their argument at all. Yet it cannot be ignored; for St. Paul was writing to a Roman Colony, and very possibly from another Roman Colony.

I think that the least hopeless expedient for those who adhere to the traditional date of 1st Corinthians is that adopted by Dr. Waite (in the *Speaker's Commentary*), who places the date of their readiness before the date of 1st Corinthians.

He writes as follows "How far the expression 'since last year' dates back is not clear, but it points to a time prior to the First Epistle, for 1st Cor. xvi. 1, 2, 4 shows that the collection was not prospering."

I have spoken of this as perhaps the least hopeless expedient for those who adopt the traditional date for 1st Corinthians; but I certainly cannot say more; for it has not an atom of foundation in 1st Corinthians xvi. St. Paul there neither asserts nor hints that the "collection was not prospering." He says nothing whatever of any previous preparedness of the Corinthians; and, of course, nothing about his having ever boasted of them to any other Church on that account. He gives no hint that they might have been more forward or that there is any danger of their unpreparedness belying the praise which he has bestowed upon them; though we know from a subsequent Epistle how skilfully and effectively he was capable of dealing with the very situation which this hypothesis supposes to exist. In this Epistle on the contrary there is no mention of any previous directions on this subject given to those to whom he is writing, but solely of directions given to the Churches of Galatia, which are now repeated to the Corinthian Church. The previous preparedness of the Corinthians and their subsequent falling off are not derived from the text, but imported into it, the sole justification being the difficulty of otherwise explaining the twice-repeated words ἀπὸ πέρυσι consistently with the late date assigned to 1st Corinthians. As for the Macedonians to whom St. Paul is supposed to have already been boasting about the Corinthians, they are not mentioned as having as yet received any directions in the matter of the collection, though they were at the time present to St. Paul's mind, for in the very next verse he mentions the fact that he intends to pass through Macedonia.

ST. PAUL'S PLANS OF TRAVEL AND THE DATE OF FIRST CORINTHIANS

I have endeavoured to trace out two lines of proof; that which treats of the intermediate visit paid by St. Paul to Corinth; and that which depends on the twice-repeated description of the time which, when he wrote his final Epistle to the Corinthians from Macedonia, had already elapsed since they could be described as ready with their contributions. These are perfectly independent of each other in their origin, but both coincide in the conclusion to which they lead, viz. that 1st Corinthians was not written in the spring of the year in which St. Paul left Ephesus, but considerably earlier, probably in the spring of the year before; that he stayed at Ephesus beyond Pentecost by reason of the greatness of the work; but that he paid a short visit to Corinth (the visit $\dot{\epsilon}\nu$ $\lambda\acute{u}\pi\eta$) and at the close of this visit promised or warned the Corinthians that he would come again, or that if he came again he would not spare.

We have now to inquire whether the notices given

20 SECOND AND THIRD CORINTHIANS

to us in the Acts and in the Epistles of the plans of travel formed by St. Paul and of the modifications of those plans as time went on, confirm or overthrow the conclusion which we have provisionally adopted.

We read in Acts xix. 21 that "Paul purposed in the spirit, when he had passed through Macedonia and Achaia, to go to Jerusalem, saying, After I have been there, I must also see Rome. And having sent into Macedonia two of them that ministered unto him, Timotheus and Erastus, he himself stayed in Asia for a while."

The formation of the Purpose to go to Jerusalem (Acts xix. 21).

The expression "Purposed in the spirit" is a remarkable one, and seems intended to describe a purpose formed with intense earnestness. The prominence which is thus given to the mention of the formation of a particular resolve by St. Paul has not received the attention which it appears to demand. Professor Ramsay has,* (I think rightly), claimed for St. Luke a place among authors of history who seize the critical events, the great crises, the great agents, and the great movements, omitting a mass of unimportant details; and we have already seen incidentally that we have in the Acts only a very small selection from the events of St. Paul's life which he himself enumerates in one of his letters. When therefore the author of the Acts makes so remarkable a departure from his usual course of chronicling

* *St. Paul the Traveller and the Roman Citizen.*

ST. PAUL'S PLANS OF TRAVEL

actions rather than purposes or feelings, he would seem to imply that the formation of the resolve to which he calls his reader's attention should be regarded as one of the critical events in the Apostle's life. Of course there are many critics who do not take Professor Ramsay's view of the historical insight of the author of the Acts; but, whatever our previous opinion may be on this point, when the historian makes such emphatic mention of this resolve, it should not be passed over lightly, but should be regarded as a possible clue which may lead to a clearer understanding of the history.

Nor have we in the first instance to engage in any elaborate research to ascertain whether the formation of this purpose is to be regarded as one of the great crises in St. Paul's history. The whole course of the events recorded from the beginning of the twentieth chapter of Acts to the end of the book was plainly determined by it. Nor are we left to infer this, for it is more than once forced on our attention by words which the writer records as having been uttered by St. Paul himself. First we have the solemn farewell at Miletus to the Elders of Ephesus in which their Apostle takes leave of them thus: "And now, behold I go bound in the spirit unto Jerusalem, not knowing the things that shall befall me there: save that the Holy Ghost testifieth unto me in every city, saying that bonds and afflictions abide me. But I hold not my life of any account, as dear unto myself, in comparison of accomplishing my course, and the ministry which I received from the Lord Jesus to testify the Gospel of the grace of God."

The words "Bound in the spirit" renew and intensify the impression of strong overmastering purpose which was first given by the words "Purposed in the spirit"; and the whole paragraph shows how firm was the Apostle's resolve; so that, though he had been warned in every city that bonds and afflictions awaited him at Jerusalem, and though these warnings gave him a feeling of apprehension which saddened his whole farewell and found its fullest expression in the almost despairing words "And now behold I know that ye all, among whom I went about preaching the Kingdom, shall see my face no more," yet he seems never for a moment to have wavered in his determination to press on towards Jerusalem.

The same combination of sorrowful apprehension with intensity of purpose appears in his reply to the announcement which Agabus made with such impressive symbolism at Caesarea, and to the unanimous entreaty of his travelling companions and of the Christians of Caesarea that he would not go up to Jerusalem: "What do ye weeping and breaking my heart? for I am ready not to be bound only, but also to die at Jerusalem for the name of

ST. PAUL'S PLANS OF TRAVEL

the Lord Jesus." We learn further that this immovable resolve at last so impressed the whole company that it prevented any further importunity; "And when he would not be persuaded, we ceased, saying, The will of the Lord be done."

This immovable resolution to allow no dangers from his enemies or entreaties of his friends to deter him from going to one particular locality has no parallel in the history of the Apostle as recorded in the Acts prior to Ch. xix. *v.* 21; indeed it stands out in sharp contrast to all the accounts which we have of his plans and movements before the formation of this resolve. Soon after his conversion his preaching at Damascus was interrupted by persecution, but he escaped and went elsewhere. It was the same at Jerusalem. When the Grecian Jews went about to kill him, the brethren brought him down to Caesarea, and sent him forth to Tarsus.

On his first missionary journey with Barnabas after they have reached the mainland we see them driven from city to city. As to leaving Antioch in Pisidia, indeed, it would appear from the narrative that no option was left to them; but from Iconium their retreat was evidently a matter of precaution when they became aware of the design of the Jews to entreat them shamefully and to stone them. In the second missionary journey, when he was accompanied by Silas, the same course was followed. When they were persecuted in one city they fled to another; from Philippi to Thessalonica, from Thessalonica to Berœa and from Berœa to Athens. Nor may we suppose that his being driven in this way from Churches which he was engaged in founding, cost St. Paul nothing; for, in the only epistles which we possess that were written soon after his visit to one of these Churches, we find him writing thus to the Thessalonians: "But we, brethren, being bereaved of you for a short season, in presence, not in heart, endeavoured the more exceedingly to see your face with great desire: because we would fain have come unto you, I Paul, once and again; and Satan hindered us."

In both these missionary journeys the plan of the Apostle clearly was to aim at the great centres of population, and among these centres to choose those in which there appeared to be an open door. While no persecution could turn him from the purpose of his life—to work for Christ—he again and again was obliged by the violence of his opponents to alter his plans with regard to the particular localities in which he had intended to work.

We find him acting in accordance with this principle even in the case of Rome. We might have conjectured that the great metropolis of the empire would have a powerful attraction for such a missionary as St. Paul, even if he had not by his own words shown us that this was actually the case; yet in the first Chapter of his Epistle to the Romans, after

ST. PAUL'S PLANS OF TRAVEL

telling them how unceasingly he has prayed that he might be prospered by the will of God to come to them, he adds "And I would not have you ignorant, brethren, that oftentimes I purposed to come to you, and was hindered hitherto"; thus showing that the same rule applied here, and the Apostle held himself ready to sacrifice his purpose should the force of circumstances seem to require it.

On the other hand, the formation of the purpose of which we read in Acts xix. 21, appears to have been a new departure, and from the day on which it was definitely adopted, his design to visit Jerusalem before proceeding to Rome seems to have been adhered to with the same intensity and fixedness with which he had all along clung to his resolve to work for the Kingdom of Christ.

It was not that St. Paul from this time forth became less ready to yield to entreaty or advice, more determined to resist any modification of purposes which he had once formed. On the contrary he continued to show on all points, other than the resolve to go to Jerusalem, the same willingness as before to listen to the advice of his friends, and to allow his plans to be altered by the force of circumstances. During the riot at Ephesus his first wish was to enter the theatre; but the disciples, and some of the Asiarchs who were his friends, advised him against this course, and St. Paul allowed himself to be overruled. Again, when he was about to sail from Corinth to Syria, it was in some way ascertained that a plot had been formed against him by the Jews, (probably to murder him in the ship), and he at once submitted to an important alteration of his plan, going round by Macedonia instead of directly by sea, but still towards the same fixed goal—Jerusalem.

If we inquire why this goal was now sought with such persistency, we shall not find any explanation given by the Author of the Acts speaking in his own person; but from utterances by St. Paul which he has recorded we may learn so much as this—*i.e.* that the Apostle regarded his journey to Jerusalem at that time as being in some way essential to the discharge of his ministry. This he shows clearly by words already quoted from his address to the Ephesian Elders: "But I hold not my life of any account, as dear unto myself, so that I may accomplish my course, and the ministry which I received from the Lord Jesus, to testify the Gospel of the grace of God." What is the meaning of these words? St. Paul's companions in travel, and the Christians of the cities through which he passed, did not seek to dissuade him from public preaching, or from going to Rome, or Spain, or to any of the cities of Europe or Asia, one only excepted. Their prayer was confined to one point—that he would not go up to Jerusalem. His words, therefore, must mean

ST. PAUL'S PLANS OF TRAVEL

that this very journey which they besought him to forego was in some way a condition necessary to the accomplishment of his course and the ministry which he had received of the Lord Jesus.

If we press our inquiry further and seek to ascertain why the journey to Jerusalem was at this time essential to the accomplishment of the ministry of the Apostle of the Gentiles, we may indeed gather from St. James's words that many of the Christians of Jerusalem had heard an unfavourable report of St. Paul's teaching and practice, and we may further gather from St. Paul's subsequent action that he was earnestly desirous of removing this unfavourable impression; but we have in the Acts no mention of the fact that the opinion formed of him in Jerusalem had produced injurious results among the Gentile Churches. The Author of the Acts does not appear to have been with St. Paul during any part of the controversy with Corinth,* and that controversy is not once mentioned in his pages. This, however, renders it only the more noteworthy that he does indirectly furnish us with a most important clue, by

---

* The "We" (instead of "They") which denotes the presence of the author with St. Paul does not appear in the narrative from the time of St. Paul's first departure from Philippi after his deliverance from prison there, to the time when he again set out from Philippi, but in the opposite direction, on his journey to Jerusalem. We find it in Chapter xvi. verse 17, immediately before the arrest of Paul and Silas; and we do not meet it again till Chapter xx. verse 5—"These going before tarried for *us* at Troas."

attending to which we can perceive the close connection which existed between the troubles at Corinth and the formation of the solemn purpose which is so remarkable a feature in the twentieth and twenty-first chapters of the Acts. For the time at which St. Luke places the adoption of this purpose by St. Paul was the very time when (as we learn from quite independent sources of information) he was in much affliction and anguish of heart, caused by the defection of the Corinthian Church.

The total omission by the Author of the Acts of any mention of the Corinthian controversy makes it most improbable that in writing Acts xix. 21 he had any deliberate intention of showing the connection between that controversy and the purpose to go to Jerusalem, and suggests that the light which this passage throws upon that connection arises simply from the fact that it states truly the time when the purpose was formed. I think that this consideration is confirmed by the fact that the phrase " Purposed in the spirit" is characteristically Pauline,* so that all the phenomena appear to indicate that the correspondence which has been already noted between the phrases "Purposed in the spirit" and "I go bound in the spirit" in Acts xx. 22, is not to be accounted for by supposing that Luke has placed the latter phrase in the mouth of Paul in Acts xx. 22,

* Cf. Rom. i. 9; 1 Cor. v. 3, 4; vi. 20; xvi. 18; Phil. iii. 3.

ST. PAUL'S PLANS OF TRAVEL

but rather that Paul has supplied the former phrase to the pen of Luke for Acts xix. 21.

The Epistle to the Romans can be shown by internal evidence to have been written after the occurrence of the events recorded in the nineteenth chapter of the Acts, so that it is natural to inquire whether it affords an opportunity of testing the accuracy of the description given in the Acts of the strength of St. Paul's purpose, and at the same time of the strain and burden of spirit which seemed to oppress him when he contemplated this journey to Jerusalem. Nor are we disappointed in our expectation of finding further guidance in our inquiry; for this Epistle furnishes conclusive proof that in neither of these points has the Author of the Acts been guilty of the slightest exaggeration.

And first as to the strength of the purpose to go to Jerusalem. I have already referred to one of the passages in the first chapter of Romans in which the writer refers to his longing to pay a visit to Rome. His language in this chapter shows unmistakably how dear this plan was to his heart. In the fifteenth Chapter he again refers to it with equal earnestness and emphasis, and discloses to his readers the fact that he has cherished this longing for many years. Yet without hesitation he pushes into the background this cherished project, and adds "But now I go to Jerusalem." The strength of a purpose is shown in a very practical way by the self-denial which it involves.

Nor does he allow us to imagine that the pleasure of accompanying to Jerusalem those who bore the bounty of the Gentile Churches, compensated him for the joy which he had looked forward to in his visit to Rome. On the contrary, he shows us in the following verses that he not only had the gravest apprehensions of the hostility of the multitude of unbelieving Jews who would be assembled in Jerusalem for the feast, but was also doubtful and anxious about the way in which the offered gifts would be received by the believing Jews. And here the strain and burden of spirit of which there are so many traces in St. Luke's history, appear in this Epistle in a very striking way. The thirtieth, thirty-first and thirty-second verses of the Chapter are such an entreaty for intercessory prayer on his behalf as has no parallel in the whole range of his Epistles. "Now I beseech you, Brethren, for the Lord Jesus Christ's sake, and for the love of the Spirit, that ye strive together with me in your prayers to God for me; that I may be delivered from them which do not believe in Judea; and that my service which I have for Jerusalem may be accepted of the saints; that I may come unto you with joy by the will of God, and may with you be refreshed." At Rome he looks for joy and refreshment, at Jerusalem bonds and afflictions seem to await him; and yet he never

ST. PAUL'S PLANS OF TRAVEL

hesitates in the resolve that to Jerusalem he must first go.

The result of the foregoing inquiry appears to be that the statement contained in Acts xix. 21 is confirmed not only by the consideration that something of the kind is required to account for the succeeding history, but also by a remarkable passage in the Epistle to the Romans, as well as by the apparently undesigned coincidence of the time assigned for the formation of the purpose to go to Jerusalem with the date of the crisis at Corinth; of which crisis the Author of the Acts makes no mention. A statement which is thus confirmed would have a strong claim to be treated as historical, even if we had started with a prejudice against the writer.

If Acts xix. 21 be admitted to be historical it furnishes a new text for the question at issue about the date of 1st Corinthians; for one of the rival theories would place the composition of that epistle before, and the other would place it after the formation of St. Paul's resolve. If the earlier date be the true one there should be a marked contrast between 1st Corinthians on the one hand, and the Epistle to the Romans and the speeches in the Acts on the other, both in the plans themselves and in the tone and spirit of the utterances concerning them which we find in these writings.

Acts xix. 21. This furnishes a new text for determining the date of 1st Corinthians.

32 SECOND AND THIRD CORINTHIANS

There is this marked contrast. In 1st Corinthians xvi. 3, 4 St. Paul shows that when he wrote 1st Corinthians he was hesitating between two alternatives, and that among these alternatives Jerusalem held only the second place. The plan which he puts forward first is that of sending on the delegates with letters of introduction to Jerusalem. It does not matter whether we suppose these letters to be written by the Churches, or (as I incline to think) by St. Paul. In either case, by saying "I will send them ($\pi\acute{\epsilon}\mu\psi\omega$) he shows that he contemplates the possibility of his not going with them himself. He adds however, as it were by an after-thought, "Or if it be meet for me to go also, they shall go with me." Nor is this his only utterance on the subject in this chapter. A little later he again shows them that he is doubtful about the direction in which he will travel when he shall have finally left them; for he says "But with you it may be that I shall abide or even winter, that ye may set me forward on my journey whithersoever I go."

It seems to me that between these utterances and the later utterances of intense feeling and immovable resolve there must have intervened a turning-point, a mental crisis like that which appears to be indicated in Acts xix. 21.

I touched briefly on this matter in an article in the *Expositor* in October 1898, and a learned and able biblical scholar, the Rev. Newport White, in a reply in the following February met it by observing that if 1st Corinthians was sent, as Mr. White believed it to have been, with much uncertainty in the writer's mind as to its probable effect, it was not to be expected that St. Paul would clearly disclose all the details of his future movements.

I agree with my critic in thinking that if 1st Corinthians were (as he supposes) the letter written with anguish at the time of the defection of the Corinthian Church, St. Paul would not have been disposed to communicate to the rebels all the details of his future movements; but I cannot think it likely that he would in that case judge it necessary, or advisable, that he should seem to take them into his confidence, and communicate to them half-formed plans and alternatives between which he was hesitating, (which is in truth a greater mark of confidence than the communication of plans which have been finally decided on), and that by doing so he should convey to them an erroneous impression. If he wished not to disclose his plans, there was a simple and dignified way of securing this, *i.e.* by saying nothing whatever about them.*

* I hope to show later on that this simple and dignified course is in fact that which appears to have been adopted by St. Paul; for I shall endeavour to prove that we have in our possession the last four chapters of the epistle which he wrote to the Corinthians "out of much affliction"; and in these the only reference which he makes to his future movements is a warning that if he comes again he will not spare. He did not condescend to add any information about the direction in which he proposed to travel when he should have finished that stern visit.

THE ABANDONED INTENTION

The generally accepted explanation of 2nd (3rd) Corinthians i. 15, 16 is as follows. That the plan there sketched out was the original plan of the Apostle for visiting Corinth; and that before he wrote our 1st Corinthians he had made a promise to the Corinthian Church to pay them the visit which is there referred to as a double benefit. That at the time when he wrote 1st Corinthians he altered his plan and postponed his visit in order to spare the Corinthians; and that by the plan which he propounded in 1st Corinthians xvi. he cancelled his earlier promise. That this revocation of a promise was made by his opponents in Corinth into an occasion for bringing against him the charge of lightness, and that it is against this charge of breaking his promise that he defends himself in 2nd Corinthians i. iv.

This interpretation has met with almost universal acceptance, and the events which it seems to disclose have apparently taken their place in the opinion of most biblical scholars among the well-ascertained facts of St. Paul's life. If we inquire into the reason of this, we shall, I think, find that the cause

THE ABANDONED INTENTION

of the favour in which this interpretation is held is the recognition by commentators of the fact that otherwise it would be impossible, on the hypothesis of the late date assigned to 1st Corinthians, to suggest any conceivable reason for the accusation of lightness brought against St. Paul. According to that hypothesis he carried out to the letter the programme which he had sketched out in 1st Corinthians xvi.; and, if any unreasonable persons had attempted to deny this, they could have been triumphantly refuted by calling attention to the express statements of that chapter. The current explanation of 2nd Corinthians i. 15, 16 gets over this difficulty by making it appear that the cause of complaint was earlier, and rested on an earlier promise which the programme in 1st Corinthians is alleged to have superseded.

Let us now test this interpretation by looking at the language of the passage from which it professes to be derived.

In that passage (if we confine ourselves to the meaning of the Greek words used by the writer) we shall find no mention of any promise. Ἐβουλόμην does not mean "I promised" but "I was wishing" and the literal translation of the passage is "And in this confidence I was wishing to go to you first, that you might have a second benefit—both to pass by you into Macedonia, and again from Macedonia to come to you—and by you to be set forward on my journey into Judea.* Did I show lightness when I was wishing this?"

The simplest explanation of these words seems to me to be, that St. Paul was telling the Corinthians of a wish which he had cherished, and of which they had not been told till now. In short the mention of this wish is not the rehearsal of an accusation which had been brought by the Corinthians, but is the writer's answer to the accusation of ἐλαφρία. Ἐλαφρία does not mean change of mind; but rather the lightness of character of a man who has no mind to change, who makes a promise without any real intention of fulfilling it, or, if he does at the time intend to do so, forgets it almost as soon as it is made, and never afterwards gives the matter a second thought. St. Paul's answer to this charge seems to be, that, while the Corinthians supposed him to be careless about them, he was all the time wishing and planning to visit them, if only he could do so without having to exercise severity. According to this interpretation he gives a clear and complete answer to the accusation; but on the received interpretation he only rehearses the objection, and then, before he has given any answer to it, demands

* The decided mention of Judea as his goal after he should have left Corinth seems to indicate a later stage in the Apostle's plans than that which is disclosed in 1st Corinthians; it may indeed be contended that this arises from his unconsciously using phraseology derived from his present purpose, but we have no right to make this assumption unless we can show some proof that this was really an earlier stage.

THE ABANDONED INTENTION

"Did I show lightness?" It is to be noted also that he takes great pains to show the advantages of this discarded plan, that he emphasises the fact that they would have received two visits, and calls it a double benefit. This is intelligible and is most apposite to his purpose, if he is vindicating himself by showing how favourable his intentions towards them have all along been; but if he is meeting an accusation of having broken a particular promise, it would indeed be a strange way of meeting it, to dwell on the advantages which that promise would have brought them if he had kept it. I think that this distinction between his answer to the accusation and the accusation itself, explains the distinction which is evidently intended to be marked between the words βουλόμενος and ἃ βουλεύομαι in the seventeenth verse (which seems to have puzzled some copyists so that they removed it, substituting βουλευόμενος for βουλόμενος). The ἃ βουλεύομαι refers, I think, to St. Paul's fixed determination to visit the Corinthians as soon as possible, the βουλόμενος to a wish which he had felt to carry out this determination in a particular way; which wish he now mentioned in order to show that the determination itself had not been lightly formed or entertained by him.

The hypothesis that St. Paul is in this passage apologising for not having fulfilled a promise to pay this double visit (which he is supposed to have made some time before he wrote 1st Corinthians, and to have revoked by substituting for it the programme which we find in that Epistle) has been received with favour by every writer in this country (so far as I know) who has expressed any opinion on the subject, and it has never been subjected to the test of serious discussion. There is however one objection to it which is so obvious that it must have forced itself on the attention of its warmest advocates. I allude to the fact that, whereas in 2nd (3rd) Corinthians the writer twice most solemnly assured his readers that it was to spare them that he had not come again to Corinth, and called God for a witness upon his soul to attest the truth of what he was writing, in 1st Corinthians he had given an entirely different reason for not going to the Corinthians at once, alleging the importance of the work at Ephesus as the reason why he must remain there till Pentecost. The only explanation I have ever seen given of this discrepancy is that St. Paul, when he was writing 1st Corinthians, did not wish to reveal his real reason and therefore substituted another.

This is the second time that we have met with a reply of this kind. I think it cannot have occurred to some writers on these epistles to notice how often they have been obliged to adopt this expedient in the interests of a particular theory, in order to escape the force of statements of St. Paul which would otherwise have shattered their theory. The difficulty here

THE ABANDONED INTENTION 39

is, however, a double one and the latter part has never been noticed. It is not only that they represent St. Paul as having given in 1st Corinthians a reason which was not his real one, when he need not have mentioned any reason at all; but also in 2nd (3rd) Corinthians, where he takes such pains to assure his readers what his real reason was, he seems (according to their theory) to have forgotten that he had lately given to those same readers an entirely different reason, one which had no reference to their interests, but to the interest of the work at Ephesus; and that this required some explanation. If he had really acted thus, he would have put a dangerous weapon into the hands of any of the Corinthians who might feel disposed to charge him with insincerity and double-dealing.

I think that the advocates of this theory unconsciously do almost as much injustice to St. Paul's diplomacy and powers of memory as they do to his straightforwardness. I believe that the language which he uses in 2nd (3rd) Corinthians about this subject shows that he retained clearly in his mind the words of the utterance to which he was referring; and that that utterance was none other than the announcement which he had made when he was leaving Corinth at the close of the visit ἐν λύπῃ that if he came again he would not spare.

I would ask the reader particularly to notice two points in that short announcement. Firstly the suggestion of a repetition of the visit (ἐὰν ἔλθω εἰς τὸ πάλιν); and secondly the question of sparing or not sparing. "If I come again I will not spare (οὐ φείσομαι)." Both these points are taken up in each of the passages in 2nd (3rd) Corinthians in which St. Paul vindicates himself from the charge of having made his announcement lightly. We have them both in 2nd (3rd) Cor. i. 23. "To spare you (φειδόμενος) I came not again (οὐκέτι) unto Corinth." We have them again in 2nd (3rd) Cor. ii. 1. "And I determined this for myself that I would not come unto you again (μὴ πάλιν) with sorrow." The phrase μὴ πάλιν ἐν λύπῃ is shown by the words which immediately follow it, to express in a most characteristic and delicate way his determination to spare them; for he adds, "For if I make you sorry (εἰ γὰρ ἐγὼ λυπῶ ὑμᾶς)."

This point will be discussed more fully later on, for it has far-reaching consequences which belong to a later stage of this inquiry, and affect more than the date of 1st Corinthians.

It may, however, seem to some readers that in spite of the remarkable appearance of correspondence between the words in which St. Paul here explains the non-fulfilment of a previous announcement and the words which he had uttered at the close of his visit to Corinth, there is still an antecedent improbability that that utterance can really be the one whose non-fulfilment he is explaining,

THE ABANDONED INTENTION 41

as it was a threat rather than a promise and the Corinthians themselves would scarcely have wished it to be carried out to the letter. This objection may derive increased plausibility from the fact that the general and long acceptance of the hypothesis which I have been criticising has familiarised men's minds with the notion that the Apostle is in these two passages apologising for not having carried out a promise to pay a double visit to the fulfilment of which the Corinthians had looked forward with pleasure.

I think, however, that a very little consideration ought to show us that it is far from being the case that the non-fulfilment of a threat might not need explanation, and that on the contrary, the suggestion that St. Paul had endeavoured to intimidate the Corinthians by announcing a visit which he had no real intention of paying, might furnish material for an accusation more envenomed and more mischievous in its effects on the minds of the Christians at Corinth than would be furnished by the delay of a pastoral visit because he was detained by his work elsewhere.

Why then, it may be asked, does he endeavour to refute the accusation of "lightness" by making known to the Corinthians a wish which he had cherished to pay them two visits which he evidently hoped would be pleasant visits?

I think the true explanation of this is to be found

in the fact that after the reconciliation of the Corinthian Church St. Paul shows on his part a loving desire to avoid saying anything which would needlessly wound their feelings now that they had renounced their rebellion. From beginning to end of these nine Chapters we shall not find a single instance of the use of the words "punishment" or "severity" in connection with his purposes towards the Corinthians, even when he is referring to the time of their defection; though he uses one of these words in speaking of the punishment which they themselves had inflicted upon an offender. We have already seen how he substituted the word "sorrow" for "severity" in Chapter ii. 1. Nor was it necessary here to infringe this self-imposed rule. He might indeed have met the charge of lightness by speaking of the earnestness with which he had purposed to punish them. But he might meet it quite as effectively by dwelling not on those moments when he had almost made up his mind that he must not spare; but rather on those other moments which alternated with them, when, in the confidence that they did partly (ἀπὸ μέρους) acknowledge him even then, he had cherished the hope which he now made known to them.

A TEST PASSAGE SECOND (THIRD) CORINTHIANS I. 13–16

The difference between the explanation which I have now laid before the reader, and that which will be found in most commentaries, is connected with a fundamental difference of interpretation of the passage 2nd (3rd) Cor. i. 13–16. The divergence is here so complete and extends to so many points in these three verses, that the passage seems to afford a valuable opportunity of bringing the rival interpretations to a decisive test.

The first of these verses is always rendered "For we write none other things unto you than what ye read or even acknowledge"; and these words are thus commented on in the introduction to this Epistle in the *Speaker's Commentary*. "But his purpose was also declared by letter; for in 2nd Cor. i. 13, where he repels the charge of deliberate equivocation with regard to this promised visit, he says: 'We *write** none other things except what ye *read*.' It was then in the missing letter that he gave the first written notice of this third visit. It could not have been in the First Canonical Epistle, for the plan of his journey there stated is not the

* The italics are in the *Speaker's Commentary*.

one first entertained." This verse then is held to deal with his first plan; and the acknowledgment spoken of in the words which follow in the same verse is referred back to the same comparatively early date. In the words of the learned commentator whom I have already quoted, "It is a reminder of a former and happier state of things which he desires to see restored." This is the interpretation of the verse generally adopted by commentators; but the next verse (the 14th) they refer with equal unanimity to the reconciliation brought about by Titus's mission for which St. Paul expresses such deep thankfulness in the seventh chapter. This verse is supposed to prove by the words ἀπὸ μέρους that the reconciliation was only partial after all.

Then in the fifteenth and sixteenth verses the Apostle is supposed to go back again to the subject of the original promise which had been made before he wrote 1st Corinthians and had been finally cancelled at the date of that epistle.

In criticising this interpretation I am not personally criticising the able and learned writer whose words I have quoted. His views, as I have already remarked, are those generally adopted by commentators; and I have quoted him as a prominent exponent of an interpretation which is almost universally received.

According to this interpretation, then, the thirteenth verse speaks of a former and happier state of things

A TEST PASSAGE

which had existed before 1st Corinthians was written, and of the original promise which had then been made; but in the very next verse the argument suddenly moves forward to the time of Titus's visit, and there is absolutely nothing to mark this important change of date, except a most contradictory indication in a change from the present tense to the aorist. The writer is supposed to speak of past events when he uses the present tense, and of the present when he uses the past. But this is nothing to what follows; for in the fifteenth verse we have, if we attend to the consecutive order of the text of the Epistle, the plan of the double visit attributed by St. Paul to his confidence in the partial acknowledgment of which he had spoken in the verse immediately before; yet that partial acknowledgment is supposed to have been the result of Titus's mission, and the plan is supposed to have been not only formed, but finally abandoned, before Titus was sent on his mission at all. The only possible expedient for avoiding this startling conclusion, is to skip arbitrarily over the fourteenth verse, and connect the fifteenth verse, which is in the past tense, not with the verse immediately before it which is also in the past tense, but with the penultimate verse, which is in the present tense.

Talleyrand is reported to have said of the Duke of Wellington that he spoke French "with great courage," and it is impossible to refuse a like meed of applause to this exegesis. Still I am not surprised that this Epistle, after having been subjected to treatment of this kind, should be described by a learned writer as "a trackless forest."

I do not think that the task of discovering a track through this portion of the Epistle is very difficult, if we allow our interpretation to be guided by the notes of time which the writer has given to us in the tenses which he has employed. The paragraph begins with the twelfth verse in which St. Paul explains his boasting (ἡ καύχησις ἡμῶν αὕτη).* This is often interpreted as if St. Paul were telling the Corinthians what he glories in; but when he wants to express this idea

---

* I agree with Meyer in holding that αὕτη is to be taken with ἡ καύχησις ἡμῶν, and that τὸ μαρτύριον κ.τ.λ. is the predicate which is introduced by ἐστί, and that ὅτι κ.τ.λ. is the content of the testimony. In confirmation of this view Meyer adduces 1 Cor. viii. 9: ἡ ἐξουσία ὑμῶν αὕτη. To this I would add that the demonstrative pronoun is so closely followed by the neuter noun τὸ μαρτύριον that, if it were the predicate here, we should expect τοῦτο instead of αὕτη. In iii. 6 we have also ἡ ἐπιτιμία αὕτη corresponding to ἡ καύχησις ἡμῶν αὕτη here. Another passage which I would refer to is 2 Corinthians xi. 10, where we have the actual phrase, ἡ καύχησις αὕτη—ἡ καύχησις αὕτη οὐ φραγήσεται εἰς ἐμὲ ἐν τοῖς κλίμασι τῆς Ἀχαίας. I doubt if there is any other sentence in this Epistle which would cause the Corinthians so much pain as this, or which would be more likely to be touched on in the communication which they seem to have made to St. Paul through Titus. In this light the occurrence of the same phrase, ἡ καύχησις αὕτη, in 2 Corinthians xi. 10 and in 3 Corinthians i. 12, becomes very significant, and seems to indicate that in the latter passage St. Paul was explaining to the Corinthians that the assertion which had wounded their feelings was a defence of his own integrity and purity of motive, and was not intended as a slight to them.

in the fourteenth verse he correctly employs the word καύχημα which seems to show that he uses καύχησις here in its proper sense, which, as Meyer* rightly observes, is not *materies gloriandi*, but *gloriatio*, the act of boasting. Nor need we depart from the correct sense of this word in order to obtain an intelligible meaning for the passage.

In two other passages in this Epistle the writer employs language which appears to indicate that in some previous communication he has commended himself. I refer to Chapter iii. 1, where the question "Do we begin *again* to commend ourselves?" seems to imply that the Apostle has been commending himself, but is not going to do so again; and to verse 12, where the assurance which in the former passage was implied by the form of the question is more expressly made in the words "We commend not ourselves *again* unto you." The occurrence of the word "again" (πάλιν) in both these passages appears to indicate that the writer has commended himself on some former occasion, though he is not going to repeat it.

These two passages, I think, give us the true clue to the meaning of Chapter i. verse 12, in which St. Paul explains his self-commendation (ἡ καύχησις) and maintains that it is simply a vindication of

* Meyer supposes that the boasting is contained in the eleventh verse of the first chapter of 2nd Corinthians.

the disinterestedness and honesty which have characterised his work and ministry in the world and especially among them. As a proof of this he appeals to their own consciousness that he has said nothing which they do not themselves acknowledge, which they would not themselves say for him. He speaks of this acknowledgment of himself by the Corinthian Christians without adding any qualifying or limiting phrase so long as he speaks in the present tense. He hopes also that they will thus acknowledge him to the end, and here again he speaks absolutely. It is very significant that it is only when the tense changes to the aorist in the fourteenth verse, that the limitation, $\dot{a}\pi\dot{o}\ \mu\epsilon\rho o\upsilon s$, makes its appearance. The mention of the present and the future seems to have suggested to him the thought of their attitude in the past. Can he say that they acknowledged him in that time of painful misunderstanding? He feels that to some extent he can even do this; but truth forbids him to speak any longer without qualification, and he therefore adds "As also (or 'even') ye did acknowledge me in part." The aorist, I need scarcely remind my readers, does not carry on the action or state to the present time, as the perfect does.

The word $\kappa\alpha i$ appears intended to emphasise the statement made in the fourteenth verse, and to mark it as being a real addition to what has been said in the verse that goes before it; yet if we neglect

A TEST PASSAGE

the change of tense, it becomes difficult to see how the strictly qualified and limited assertion which he now makes can add anything to the stronger statement which has preceded it. The change to the aorist explains the meaning of the writer's insertion of the καί, for it shows that he is making an important addition to what he has already said. He is now asserting that even in the past they did partly acknowledge him.

The paragraph began with the word καύχησις and the keynote of the concluding sentence in it is the cognate word καύχημα indicating that the καύχησις has been the subject all through. This concluding statement gives the substance of all the acknowledgments, of the present, and of the future, and of the partial acknowledgment in the past. The connecting link between it and the καύχησις of the twelfth verse is the assertion in the thirteenth verse that everything which he has said in self-commendation they would say for him; to which thought he gives final expression in the declaration that he is their boast as they are his in the day of our Lord Jesus Christ.

Then, in the fifteenth verse, he begins a new subject and tells them that in the confidence which he felt in this more hopeful view of their feelings towards him he cherished for some time (ἐβουλόμην) the wish to pay them a two-fold visit, of which he informs them in that verse. That before the reconciliation he sometimes took this comparatively favourable view of their attachment to him may also be learned from the fourteenth verse of the seventh chapter, which shows that he had boasted of them to Titus when he was sending him on his mission. This boasting was indeed justified by the event, for the account which we have of the Corinthians' reception of Titus seems to show that before his arrival they were partly at least prepared for submission. König* has remarked that St. Paul's visit, and departure, and departing warning may have produced more impression than he himself at the time was aware of.

Schmiedel in his comments on this passage† has noticed the apparent incongruity of the introduction of a detail like the supposed reference to the plan of a double visit in the midst of the wide and general statement which the writer is making in the twelfth verse; and has also remarked that it is a very insufficient proof of that general statement, (though, for a reason which I shall presently notice, he considers that he is obliged to adopt this interpretation of the sentence). I may add that the words thus interpreted would be an equally insufficient answer to the specific accusation to which they are supposed to be a reply. If St. Paul were charged with non-fulfilment of a specific promise,

* *Zeitschrift für Wissenschaftliche Theologie*, October, 1897.
† *Hand-Commentar zum Neuen Testament*, Zweiter Band, Erste Abtheilung, S. 213.

A TEST PASSAGE

it would be no answer to say "We write none other things unto you than what you read," when the gist of the objection is supposed to be, that he did not keep the promise which he wrote and they read.

I may be told that I have no right to assume that St. Paul must have given an adequate answer to any objection. I should admit the force of this, if the objection were actually found in the text. But I maintain that when commentators construct a hypothetical objection to account for a sentence in the text, which is supposed to be a reply to it; the hypothesis loses its *raison d'être* if it can be shown that the sentence in question would not be any answer to it at all.

INTERPRETATION OF "'Ἀναγινώσκετε" IN SECOND (THIRD) CORINTHIANS I. 13; AND OF "'Ἀναγινωσκομένη" IN III. 2

Before the time of Pindar the most usual meaning of ἀναγινώσκω or ἀναγιγνώσκω was, to know again, to recognise, to acknowledge. Pindar is the first writer who is known to have given it the signification "to read"; (γράμματα being understood); but this sense is from his time the most frequent in Attic Greek; and of course from the nature of the case prevailed especially in literary circles. The old meaning did not at once die out but remained side by side with the later technical sense. From the nature of the case this older use would continue longest among non-literary populations whose mother tongue was Greek. There indeed it would naturally be the predominant use, long after the literary meaning had become the prevalent one in books. The word is used by St. Paul in 2nd (3rd) Cor. iii. 15 to express this later meaning "to read"; and, by the unanimous consent of all commentators, it is supposed to be employed in the same sense here.

The ancient meaning of ἀναγινώσκετε in this passage, however, was adopted by the Peshito,

MEANING OF ΑΝΑΓΙΝΩΣΚΟΜΕΝΗ 53

which renders the word by yod'in. This is a significant fact, and it is strange that it has attracted so little attention. If the earlier meaning of ἀναγινώσκειν was sufficiently prevalent in the second century to be familiar to the writers who made this translation, so that they believed it to be the sense in which St. Paul used the word here, it is probable that it was at least equally prevalent when St. Paul wrote the passage, a century earlier.*

I have never seen a satisfactory explanation of the words "We write none other things unto you than what you read." It certainly cannot mean "I write none other things than what you read in the pages of other writers"; for St. Paul is one of the last authors of whom this could be said. Alford's

---

* Dr. Abbott has called my attention to the fact that the Prayer of Manasses, as edited by Robert Stephens from the Victorian manuscript, has ἀναγινώσκω in a passage in which it must mean "acknowledge": ἡμάρτηκα, Κύριε, ἡμάρτηκα, καὶ τὰς ἀνομίας μου ἀναγινώσκω. The Alexandrine manuscript of the Prayer, indeed, has ἐγὼ γινώσκω; but ἐγώ could not be emphatic here, and there is therefore no reason why it should be expressed. The Latin translation which is appended to the Vulgate has agnosco here, which appears to represent ἀναγινώσκω, rather than ἐγὼ γινώσκω. The translator of the Latin version in the Complutensian Polyglot had ἐγὼ γινώσκω before him in the Greek, and he rendered it by ego cognosco. Ἐγὼ γινώσκω was probably a conjectural emendation for ἀναγινώσκω. But if it be objected that we may, on the contrary, regard ἀναγινώσκω as a conjectural emendation, and ἐγὼ γινώσκω as the original text, this would not greatly affect the argument, for in that case it would appear that the scribe who made the emendation must have been familiar with the earlier meaning of ἀναγινώσκω. In its later meaning it would be utterly unintelligible here.

54 SECOND AND THIRD CORINTHIANS

explanation is as follows. "My character in my writings is one and the same, not fickle and changing, but such as past facts have substantiated it to be, and as I hope future facts to the end of my life will continue to do." The interpretation given in the *Speaker's Commentary* is not unlike this. "He re-asserts his sincerity," for "it is not true that his letters have any other sense than that which presents itself on the simple reading, or any at variance with what they well knew of him personally." Klöpper in his commentary gives a somewhat similar paraphrase of the passage.*

These explanations agree with each other in seeking to find an intelligible meaning for the words in question by representing them as making some assertion about the character of St. Paul's writings—their consistency or their clearness of meaning—rather than about any action, mental or otherwise, of the Corinthians. This might be a possible explanation if the sentence ended with the word ἀναγινώσκετε; but, as it is, the context excludes it. The relative (ἅ) is governed not only by ἀναγινώσκετε but also by a series of verbs, which are joined by

* "Wir machen euch brieflich keine anderen Mittheilungen als solche die sich sofort beim Lesen als das herausstellen, was der Wortlaut besagt, oder von denen Ihr etwa durch Vergleichung mit meiner sonstigen Sinnes - Denk - und Handlungsweise die Ueberzeugung gewinnt, das sie der adaquäte Ausdruck meines innersten Bewusstseins sind."—*Kommentar über das zweite Sendschreiben des Apostel Paulus auf die Korinther*, S. 133.

MEANING OF ΑΝΑΓΙΝΩΣΚΟΜΕΝΗ

conjunctions to ἀναγινώσκετε and to each other. Each of these verbs is in the second person plural, and makes some emphatic assertion about the agency, or mental state, of those whom the writer is addressing, and about that alone. "I write none other things unto you than what ye ... or even acknowledge, and I hope will acknowledge to the end." Whatever may be the character of the action which St. Paul is ascribing to the Corinthians in the verb which is to fill the place which I have left blank, its close connection with the other verbs shows that he is ascribing something to them, and is not merely making an assertion about the character of his own writings.

The words ἢ καί which connect the ἀναγινώσκετε with the ἐπιγινώσκετε show that the writer regards the latter of these verbs as standing to the former in the relation of a stronger to a weaker assertion, and that therefore, as used by him, they must be sufficiently akin to be capable of being compared in this way. Now, reading and acknowledging are not thus akin. They are not, and cannot be, related to each other as a weaker and stronger assertion. We may read with the most intense approval and belief, or with an equally intense disbelief, or in a state of mind which wavers between the two. We might therefore search the whole range either of English (or Greek) literature in vain for such an expression as "reading *or even* acknowledging." "Reading *and* acknowledging" would be the phrase invariably employed. Nor is this the only consideration which suggests that the words must be thus related to each other. I do not think any commentator has ever called attention to the fact that the basis of each of these words is the same simple verb; and that they differ from each other only in the prefix. These are facts which appear to be inexplicable under the received interpretation. I have never seen even an attempt made to explain them. If, however, we adopt the older meaning of ἀναγινώσκετε they at once become intelligible and significant; and the whole passage is seen to have a clear and connected meaning.

According to this interpretation the two words are intended to express different degrees of assent. We might endeavour to preserve the combination of the same verbal root with varying suffixes by rendering the sentence "We write none other things unto you than those to which you assent or even consent"; but, as the writer evidently regards the latter word as denoting a stronger and more active form of acknowledgment, we may perhaps better express the contrast of meaning thus—"For we write none other things unto you than what you admit or even maintain, and I hope will maintain unto the end, as also ye even did in the past partly maintain of us that we are your boast."

The use of the stronger term in speaking of the partial acknowledgment, need create no surprise; for its force is sufficiently limited by the words ἀπὸ

MEANING OF ΑΝΑΓΙΝΩΣΚΟΜΕΝΗ

μέρους. To have reverted to the weaker term, in addition to inserting this limiting phrase, would have been needlessly depreciatory; and would therefore have been at variance with the writer's evident desire to speak as favourably as truth would permit.

Schmiedel has recognised more fully than other commentators the confusion which the current interpretation brings into this verse; and he has alluded to the older meaning of ἀναγινώσκειν in such a way as to suggest that it may for a moment have presented itself to him as a possible solution of the difficulty. He rejects the solution, however, on the ground that in the New Testament ἀναγινώσκειν always signifies "to read." Meyer also (though he notices the fact that the Peshito in this place does not translate ἀναγινώσκετε in this way) confidently asserts that in the New Testament the word invariably has this meaning.

I think that this has been too hastily laid down as a canon of New Testament interpretation; and that there is another passage in this very Epistle which should have been carefully examined before this rule was so dogmatically laid down. In Ch. iii. 2, 3, in what is evidently intended to be a connected statement, ἀναγινωσκομένη is placed between two other participles, the connection between which is broken by it, if we translate it "read"; but is at once restored if we give it its older meaning "acknowledged." The first of these participles describes the Corinthian Church as being known by all men to be the Epistle of Christ; the third as being made manifest to be so; the interpolation between these two assertions of the statement that they were read by all men introduces a new idea, and interrupts in a most confusing way the connection between the γινωσκομένη and the φανερούμενοι. If on the other hand we assign to ἀναγινωσκομένη its older meaning it will be at once seen to harmonise with the other two, and complete the sense; so that the passage becomes one clear and connected statement. They were an Epistle of Christ known, and acknowledged by all men, because they were manifested to all men as being so.

Though the disturbance of the connection of this passage, to which I have endeavoured to call attention, has been passed over by all commentators in silence; there is another point which has not been altogether unnoticed by them. I refer to the strangeness of the phrase, "Known and read"; its reversal of what seems to be the natural order—"Read and known." Meyer quotes with approval Grotius's explanation "Prius agnoscitur manus deinde legitur epistola." "First the hand of the writer is recognised, afterwards the letter is read."

This holds good for letters written on paper or parchment, but not for Epistles like those of which St. Paul is speaking. Here the world may conclude from the outward life and conversation that the

Spirit has been writing within; but the fleshy tables of the heart on which the Spirit writes are not open to the eye of man and cannot be read by him.

This second difficulty, like the first, completely disappears the moment the older meaning of ἀναγινωσκομένη is adopted here. In the phrase "Known and acknowledged" the words are at once seen to be in an order which is as natural and appropriate, as "Known and read" is inappropriate.

St. Paul before the date of this Epistle had lived and worked for two years in Achaia, and had also spent some time alone at Athens, where there were very few Jews. In these places he must have been brought into intimate contact with men who might, in his own phraseology, be described as "Greeks of the Greeks"; and even if we were able to suppose that he had never previously learned the older meaning of ἀναγινώσκω he was not unlikely to meet with it there. For, from the nature of the Religion which he taught, the idea of the *acknowledgment* of truths, and of persons, was one which would recur again and again in the conversations which he held with those about him. A mind like his could not fail to be interested by what he would at once perceive to be the etymological meaning of the word. Every reader of his Epistles knows how often he was wont to illustrate what he had to say by a play on the various meanings of the words which he used; and it would therefore have been strange if he had not noted this meaning for possible future use. It is significant that on each of the two occasions on which he uses ἀναγινώσκω in its etymological sense, he specially calls attention to its etymology by placing it side by side—first with the simple verb from which it is derived, and on the second occasion, with the kindred verb ἐπιγινώσκω. On the other hand, when he uses the word in its technical sense, he never calls attention to its etymology.

I think we may also observe that, according to this hypothesis, St. Paul is consistent in his observance of the distinction of weaker and stronger which he draws between ἀναγινώσκω and ἐπιγινώσκω by his use of the word ἢ καί before the latter verb in Chap. i. 13. In 1 Cor. xvi. 18 he urges the Corinthians loyally to acknowledge those who had shown special liberality; and he there of course uses the word ἐπιγινώσκετε; but in 2nd (3rd) Cor. iii. 2 he is speaking of the outside world, (or of other Churches) who were obliged, by facts which they could not escape noticing, to recognise the Corinthian Church as the Epistle of Christ. Here the notion of active, loyal acknowledgment would plainly be quite out of place; so that ἐπιγινωσκομένη would be too strong an expression; and he is, therefore, only acting in accordance with his own rule when he substitutes ἀναγινωσκομένη as having a weaker and more passive meaning.

AGREEMENT OF THE PLAN OF TRAVEL SKETCHED IN FIRST CORINTHIANS XVI. WITH THAT WHICH WAS FINALLY ADOPTED

I think that the agreement of the plan mentioned in 1 Cor. xvi. with that which was finally adopted, has weight with many minds, and is supposed to be an important confirmation of the later date of the formation of this plan. It might fairly be thus regarded if there were several routes from Ephesus to Corinth ; but, as Schmiedel has observed,* there were only two — one by sea, the other through Macedonia — so that, if St. Paul had changed his plan more than once, then he must of necessity in every change he made fall back on one or other of his old plans. Under these circumstances the coincidence of a plan with the course which was actually followed afterwards is a very insufficient proof of the date at which it was first sketched out.

This coincidence however would have gone some way towards giving a *primâ facie* probability to the later date for this Epistle were it not for the fact that when St. Paul was writing from Macedonia

* *Hand-commentar.*

only a few months after this later date, he alluded to a charge of lightness which had been brought against him, and in replying to it did not deny that he had delayed his visit; whereas if 1st Corinthians was written in the spring of the same year he was carrying out its programme without any delay. We have already seen that in his reply to the charge he did not so much as mention the programme of 1st Corinthians, while he twice referred to the words which he had addressed to the Corinthians when he was leaving Corinth.

DESCRIPTION IN THE EPISTLE WHICH WAS WRITTEN FROM MACEDONIA TO THE CORINTHIANS OF THE LAST EPISTLE SENT TO THEM BY THE SAME WRITER

The Epistle which was written from Macedonia furnishes us with four marks for the identification of the Epistle which had been sent immediately before it. If these marks are to be found in 1st Corinthians, this circumstance may legitimately be regarded as a strong proof that it is the Epistle in question, and may be set against the proofs of its earlier date to which I have already called attention. This is a correspondence which may reasonably be expected between two Epistles written with so short an interval of time between them.

The first of these notes of identification is given to us in 2nd (3rd) Corinthians ii. 4, where the writer says "Out of much affliction and anguish of heart I wrote unto you with many tears." Emotions so intense disturbing the mind of the writer could not but leave their traces in the Epistle which was written under their influence.

To this note of identification I maintain that 1st Corinthians answers very imperfectly indeed. In the fourth verse of the first Chapter its author, after his opening salutation, gives utterance to an earnest thanksgiving which is continued for six verses. He goes on afterwards to speak of the party spirit, and of the grave disorders of the existence of which he has been informed, but in doing this he shows no traces of despondency or anguish of mind. In the midst of the portion of the Epistle which relates to these matters he turns aside to answer queries which his correspondents have addressed to him, and takes these up point by point, in a calm and business-like manner, apparently with their letter lying open before him. He begins the seventh Chapter with the words "But concerning the things about which you wrote me" (περὶ δὲ ὧν ἐγράψατε) and proceeds at some length to discuss an important question, not in a tone of reproof or controversy, but in that of a teacher answering questions of disciples who had sought guidance from him. In the twenty-fifth verse he takes up another of their enquiries (as is indicated by the recurrence of the phrase "But concerning" περὶ δὲ τῶν παρθένων) and discusses it likewise in the spirit of a calm instructor. A third point is introduced with a like formula ("But concerning things offered to idols" περὶ δὲ τῶν εἰδωλοθύτων) in the opening of the eighth Chapter, and the instruction given about it occupies the whole of that Chapter. Then comes a Chapter in which there is a more controversial tone, followed by two Chapters in which warning and instruction are blended; and then in the first verse of the twelfth Chapter we have a recurrence of the formula "But concerning" περὶ δὲ τῶν πνευματικῶν. As the opening of the Epistle was cheerful so is the closing portion; he seemed to look forward with pleasure to visiting the Corinthians, and perhaps abiding or even wintering with them; and he gives directions about the reception of Timothy and their due submission to the house of Stephanas, briefly, and simply, and with the tone of a man who is confident that his direction will have weight with those whom he regards as being in the main obedient children, in spite of their faults. From beginning to end of this Epistle there are no traces of anguish of heart and much affliction, either in utterances expressing these feelings, or in the style of the Epistle itself. Dr. Plummer, in an article in Smith's *Dictionary of the Bible*, justly says of its style that it "should possibly be ranked first among St. Paul's writings." He adds, "Possibly no such thought was in his mind; but the letter might convince the fastidious Greeks that in clearness of thought and power of language he was no way inferior to the eloquent Apollos."

In explanation of this it has been urged that St. Paul "put such chains on his feelings that his letter reflects no true image of them"; but a careful perusal of the paragraph will show that it was because his feelings had not been suppressed but had been strongly expressed that he thought it necessary that he should explain to the Corinthians that it was in sorrow rather than in anger that he had written what had caused them pain.

The second note of identification is given in 2nd (3rd) Corinthians vii. 8, 9, where the writer lets us see that his affliction had been caused by the conduct of the Corinthians and that he had expressed his sense of this so strongly in the Epistle to which he there refers, that after he had sent it to them, he for a time repented having done so, ("though I did repent," 2nd (3rd) Cor. vii. 8).

Here again 1st Corinthians corresponds very imperfectly; for though in that Epistle the writer speaks of grave faults this was only what faithfulness required. The blame occupies but a small portion of the letter, which contains also a good deal of praise and an amount of valuable instruction* which far exceeds either. The keynote of the warnings in 1st Corinthians is I think given to us in Chap. iv. 21 : "What will ye? shall I come unto you with

---

* Dr. Waite in his Introduction to this Epistle in the *Speaker's Commentary* has well remarked that "it is scarcely comprehensible that St. Paul should have said, even in a moment of strong excitement, of so costly a monument of Christian truth as the First Epistle is, that he repented for a while of ever having written it."

ST. PAUL'S DESCRIPTION

a rod, or in love, and in the spirit of meekness?" Here the form of the question seems to imply the hope that it will be in love that he will be enabled to come.

The third mark of identification may be gathered from two passages in 2nd (3rd) Corinthians, viz. iii. 1, where the question, "Do we begin *again* to commend ourselves?" seems to imply that the Apostle has been commending himself, but is not going to do so again; and the assurance that this will not be repeated which is implied here by the form of the question, is more expressly made in v. 12, "We commend not ourselves again unto you," where the repetition of the word "again" ($\pi \acute{a} \lambda \iota \nu$) seems to me to show that the writer has done this on some former occasion, but is not going to repeat what it had given him so much pain to write.

This note corresponds with 1st Corinthians a little better than the two former ones, as there is a certain amount of self-vindication in that Epistle. Still, self-commendation is not a very marked feature in it, and the greater part of the self-vindication which it contains is written with reference to the question of the Apostle's refusal to accept payment for his labours among them.

A fourth mark of identification of the Epistle referred to in 2nd (3rd) Corinthians ii. 4 is furnished by i. 23 and ii. 1, which show that St. Paul was, at the time when he wrote, contemplating, and at the same time shrinking from, a visit which must be of a severe character, and that in the end, out of mercy to them he did not pay it.

With this note of identification the references in 1st Corinthians to St. Paul's intention of visiting Corinth do not correspond at all; for he there fixes the time when he purposes to visit them without the slightest sign of hesitation, and with the sole proviso "if the Lord will" and he tells the Corinthians that his reason for not coming sooner was the absorbing nature of the work at Ephesus (1st Cor. xvi. 8, 9). He fixes his visit for the autumn and possibly the winter, so that if this Epistle was written in the same year the visit was not deferred at all. In this Chapter he also speaks of abiding with them (1 Cor. xvi. 6), as if the visit was one to which both he and they might look forward with pleasure.

This total want of correspondence in some points, partial correspondence in others, but complete correspondence in nothing, is just what might have been expected between an earlier and later stage of St. Paul's relations to the Corinthian Church, separated by an interval of a year or more. This enquiry, therefore, instead of furnishing us with proofs which might counterbalance the proofs of the earlier date of 1st Corinthians, tends rather to confirm them.

THE MISSION OF TIMOTHY TO CORINTH, AND HIS MISSION TO MACEDONIA

The mention in Acts xix. 22 of the mission of Timothy to Macedonia is regarded by Paley in his *Horæ Paulinæ* as furnishing a striking coincidence with the mention in 1st Corinthians of his mission to Corinth; and many later writers seem to consider that these statements coincide closely enough to entitle them to assume that the two documents refer to one and the same mission. Some indeed are so confident of this that they write as if they had found their theory in the text; and more than one commentator speaks of our "learning from the Acts that Timothy was sent to Corinth by way of Macedonia." This is not an inference which should be introduced without discussion as if it were on the same footing with the statements of the historian.

There is, however, one inference, which has been made by all critics who have written on this subject, to which I unreservedly subscribe. All seem to agree that Timothy was not merely sent to Corinth *viâ* Macedonia, but was entrusted with a mission to the latter place (probably in connection with the collection for Jerusalem). This appears to be a most reasonable conclusion from the words of St. Luke. If an ambassador was sent from London or Paris to St. Petersburg, and travelled thither through Germany, without delaying, or transacting business there; no historian who knew the facts would describe them by saying that his Government "sent him to Germany."

My agreement, however, with this inference forms a barrier to my yielding assent to the further inference (made by most of these writers) that Timothy was entrusted also with the mission to Corinth. When St. Paul wrote (as he has himself told us) to the Corinthian Church "out of much affliction and anguish of heart and many tears"; I cannot but think that he must have regarded the business which obliged him to write that letter as being of sufficient importance to demand the undivided time and attention of the best envoy that he could send; that it must have been the $ἔργον$ and not the $πάρεργον$ of whoever it was entrusted to. It seems evident from the words of Acts xix. 22 that he was not altogether deprived of the power of choice in such a matter; for Timothy and Erastus are there described as "two of them that waited on him." One other possible envoy at least—Titus—cannot have been very far off.

THE MISSIONS OF TIMOTHY

I think, therefore, that even if we had no other evidence, and were confined to two documents—1st Corinthians, and the Book of "the Acts"—the balance of probability would be in favour of the conclusion that the mission to Corinth was not entrusted to Timothy at the same time as the mission to Macedonia.

But there is another document whose total silence about any mission of Timothy to Corinth at the later date, throws a heavy weight into the same scale. According to the traditional theory, 1st Corinthians was the Epistle which was written with tears from Ephesus, and was therefore the very Epistle about which so much is said in the earlier part of 2nd Corinthians where its effect upon the minds of the Corinthian Christians is described.

It is admitted therefore by every writer on this subject that they should have expected beforehand to find the mission of Timothy a prominent topic in the latter Epistle, as it had been expressly announced in the former one. "For this cause have I sent unto you Timothy, who is my beloved and faithful child in the Lord, who shall put you in remembrance of my ways which be in Christ, even as I teach everywhere in every Church."

Nevertheless, the ingenuity of all the commentators who have written on 2nd Corinthians has never been able to discover in it the slightest allusion to any mission of Timothy to Corinth at the time when the

Epistle there spoken of was sent, or to any news brought by him from Corinth to Macedonia; though the original preaching of the Gospel at Corinth by Timothy as well as by Paul and Silas is referred to in the nineteenth verse of the first Chapter; and what makes this silence even more remarkable is the circumstance that the place in this Epistle which we should have expected to have been filled by Timothy is not left vacant, but is filled by Titus, whose name is introduced abruptly, and without explanation, in the thirteenth verse of the second Chapter, in such a way as to show that the writer felt that every Corinthian reader was prepared for the reference to him as the bringer of news to Macedonia.

In every reference in this Epistle to the repentance of the Corinthians or to the mission which led to it, Titus alone is spoken of as the agent of St. Paul and no hint is given indicating that there had been any other envoy.

Some explanation of what appears to be a strange omission has been felt to be necessary, and three distinct theories have been framed to account for it. The first of these theories, (which has the support of such writers as Bertholdt, Credner, De Wette, Maier, Neander, Reuss, and Ziegler), endeavours to account for the silence of 2nd Corinthians by supposing that Timothy had regarded the mission to Corinth so much in the light of a πάρεργον that he had spent all his time

THE MISSIONS OF TIMOTHY

in Macedonia, and had not gone on to Corinth at all; but that, having finished his mission in Macedonia, he had returned to Paul at Ephesus. Against this theory Meyer objects that since Timothy was (according to 1st Corinthians iv. 17) so distinctly delegated to Corinth, we are not justified in believing that he left the Apostolic mission unfulfilled, or that Paul himself had cancelled it; otherwise we should necessarily expect the Apostle in his Second Epistle to have explained to his readers *why* Timothy had not come; especially as the anti-Pauline party would not have failed to turn the non-appearance of Timothy to account in their controversy.

The second theory is that of Eichhorn who held that Timothy had finished his visit to Corinth and left it again before the arrival of our First Epistle in that city. To this Meyer objects "that it presupposes that the bearers of the first Epistle lingered on the journey (1st Cor. xvi. 17), which there is the less ground to assume as these men presumably had no other aim than to return from Ephesus to Corinth." Indeed the supposition of gross negligence on the part of one or other of St. Paul's messengers is a vital element in all these theories. None of them can dispense with it.

The third hypothesis which has been framed in explanation of the silence of 2nd Corinthians about the mission of Timothy to Corinth is, I think, the one which is most generally accepted, and it has the support of Meyer whose forcible objections to the other explanations have just been quoted. According to this theory, Timothy having discharged his commission in Macedonia went on to Corinth, and endeavoured to enforce the message of 1st Corinthians, but failed, and returned to St. Paul to Ephesus to inform him of the unfavourable reception of his letter.

This explanation, indeed, avoids making the improbable supposition that Timothy left Corinth prematurely instead of waiting till the important letter arrived; but it avoids this only to come into collision with St. Paul's distinct assertion that it was the letter which made the Corinthians sorry: "For though I made you sorry with my Epistle, I do not regret it though I did regret, for I see that that Epistle made you sorry, though but for a season." According to this account, though the letter came to the Corinthian Church at the time of Timothy's visit or before it, it remained without effect; and it was not till he had journeyed back to Ephesus and Titus had been sent to take his place that they repented. The haste too with which, according to this theory, Timothy must be supposed to have left Corinth, in order to bring all the events within the short space of time between spring and summer, is another difficulty. He is represented as first spending time in Macedonia, then after completing his task there, attempting to

THE MISSIONS OF TIMOTHY

hurry through the vitally important negotiations at Corinth, then hastening back to St. Paul to report his failure, thus leaving time for a new envoy to be sent to make good his failure. If we had read all this in the narrative we must have accepted it as an account of the order of events, though we might have thought it a strange method of conducting so critical and delicate a negotiation. But there is not a word of it in the text, except the statement that Timothy was sent into Macedonia. All the rest is a purely imaginary narrative constructed by advocates of the later date of 1st Corinthians to explain the total (and for them highly inconvenient) silence of 2nd Corinthians about any mission of Timothy to the Corinthians at the time of their rebellion.

Dr. Waite in the *Speaker's Commentary*, and the celebrated German critics Schmiedel and Klöpper, adopt in the main what I believe to be the true solution, for they abandon the attempt to represent 1st Corinthians to be the Epistle which caused the repentance of the Corinthians; though they seem to me to involve their account of the matter in needless difficulty by retaining too much of the traditional view, and dating 1st Corinthians after the intermediate visit of St. Paul to Corinth. The *Speaker's Commentary* supposes the date of 1st Corinthians and of the mission of Timothy to have been only a few weeks earlier than that of the severe Epistle and of the mission of Titus.

I believe that the earlier date of 1st Corinthians (which is established, as I have endeavoured to show, by so many independent lines of proof) gives us the true explanation of the silence of 2nd (3rd) Corinthians about the mission of Timothy to Corinth. Once that date is accepted we no longer expect to find any allusion to his mission in an Epistle which we now know to have been written a year later, especially as St. Paul himself had paid a short visit to Corinth in the interval. But the missions of Timothy and Titus to Corinth were not only separated by an interval of time, they were also to some extent different in their aim, and this circumstance explains the difference in the Apostle's choice of envoys on the two occasions. This difference in the character of the missions will be apparent if we attend to the account given in 1st Corinthians of the mission to Corinth with which Timothy was entrusted. The charge given to the Corinthians "See that he be with you without fear, for he worketh the work of God, as I also do" would have been a strange introduction of an envoy to rebels whom he had been commissioned to bring to their knees. It was appropriate to the case of one who was young and of a retiring disposition, but who was able to give the Corinthians valuable instruction about St. Paul's ways and his teaching in every Church. For this there was probably no other envoy that could have been found who was

THE MISSIONS OF TIMOTHY

so well fitted as Timothy, and this is expressly stated in 1st Corinthians iv. 17 to have been the object for which Timothy was then sent. "Be ye imitators of me. For this cause have I sent unto you Timothy, who is my beloved and faithful child in the Lord, who shall put you in remembrance of my ways which be in Christ, even as I teach everywhere in every Church." Some of his instruction no doubt would be about things of which they should not have been ignorant; but we have already seen that there are indications in 1st Corinthians that the Corinthian Church had asked for additional information concerning several points in St. Paul's teaching.

It was no slight to Timothy if a year later a new envoy was selected for a new mission to Corinth. The situation had changed in the interval, and assumed a critical character which made it advisable that the man who was sent to deal with it should have very special qualifications. St. Paul, therefore, whose insight into character was not obscured even by his love, allotted to Timothy the loyal province of Macedonia, while he entrusted Corinth to Titus.

Part II.

THE IDENTIFICATION

IF 1st Corinthians is not the letter which was referred to by St. Paul in the Epistle which he wrote to Corinth from Macedonia, the question at once arises, Has that letter then been lost? I shall now state some reasons which have led me to the conclusion that it has not totally perished, but that the concluding portion of it has all along been preserved in our Bibles, having been placed by those who copied the original manuscript at the end of the very letter in which reference is made to it, so that in the document which appears in our Canon as 2nd Corinthians there are really two Epistles, of which the last written stands first.

The first comment of most readers will probably be, that it would take very strong proof to convince them of such a theory. This is a reasonable comment, and I shall add to it the statement that the theory is one which from the nature of the case should, if it be true, be capable of being established by strong proofs of various kinds. Not only should there be so marked a difference of *tone* and spirit as to present great difficulty to all readers who regard the document as one whole; but also, (unless the transition was bridged by an alteration of the text) there should be a sudden break in the *sense* at the place where one letter ends and another begins. In addition to this, the fact that these two Epistles must have been written by the same writer, to the same Church, and with only a short interval between them, and that, if they be really separate Epistles, they must refer to the same circumstances seen from very different standpoints, makes it highly probable that if the theory be true, there ought to be passages in which the Epistle which was written later refers back either to the very phraseology of passages in the earlier Epistle, or to the acts and purposes there spoken of. I shall begin with some references of this kind, which I regard as the most important proofs, because they are of the nature of positive evidence.

In the second Chapter of the Epistle which was written from Macedonia and which I have designated 3rd Corinthians St. Paul three times expressly mentions the Epistle which he had written a short time before to the Corinthians from Ephesus. In the third verse he explains one of the objects for which he wrote it; in the fourth verse he tells them what his mental state was at the time when it was being written; and in the ninth verse he informs them of another object which he had in view in writing

THE IDENTIFICATION

it, which object was however intimately connected with that which is referred to in the third verse.

The first identification is furnished by the first of these passages. In verse 3, writing in the past tense, he says, "And I wrote this same thing that when I came I might not have sorrow."

If we now turn to 2nd Corinthians xiii. 10, we there find him using the present tense when he says "For this cause I write these things while absent that I may not when present deal sharply."

The parallelism is complete but for one apparent discrepancy. In the passage where he writes in the present tense St. Paul says "That I may not use sharpness," but when he speaks in the past tense he says "That I might not have sorrow." This apparent discrepancy is, however, converted into a coincidence full of significance by the fact that in the verses which immediately precede we are shown that "sorrow" is in this paragraph an euphemism for "severity"; for the expression in the first verse "Come unto you in sorrow" is, as we have already seen, shown to be an euphemism of this kind, by the reason given in the second verse for the determination not to come to them again in sorrow, "For if *I make you sorry* who is he then that maketh me glad but the same that is made sorry by me?" This fixes the meaning of "sorrow" for us in this paragraph, so that the "That I might not have sorrow" of the third verse is seen to be the equivalent of "That I may not use sharpness" in the thirteenth Chapter of 2nd Corinthians.

Now, when his Corinthian Christians have repented, and when he is able to speak of the time of estrangement in the past tense, St. Paul seems to dislike speaking of using severity, even when he is explaining that he had shrunk from it, and had endeavoured successfully to avoid using it. It is to be noted that the words "severity," "sharpness," and "punishment" are never once found in these nine Chapters in connection with the purposes of St. Paul.

The paragraph from which the first of this pair of corresponding sentences is taken, is the very paragraph in which the Apostle is speaking of having written out of much affliction, so that unless the correspondence be merely apparent, it is a direct identification of 2nd Corinthians xii. 10 as part of the Epistle referred to in 3rd Corinthians ii. 4 as written ἐκ πολλῆς θλίψεως.

The second passage which I shall adduce as referring to words in 2nd Corinthians, is to be found in 3rd Corinthians i. 23, "To spare you I came not again unto Corinth."

This is one of the two passages in which St. Paul, following up his vindication of himself from the charge of lightness, explains his reasons for not having paid a visit which he had previously an-

THE IDENTIFICATION

nounced. We have already seen that each of these two passages (i. 23 and ii. 1) takes up two points which are to be found in the announcement made by the Apostle when leaving Corinth ("If I come again I will not spare"), viz., the question of a repetition of the visit, and the question of sparing or not sparing. But I have now to call attention to the fact that that announcement was adopted and repeated by St. Paul in 2nd Corinthians xiii. 2 as expressing his intention at the time when he was writing, and that he then endeavoured to impress on the minds of the Corinthians the fact that he was repeating by a letter, in his absence from them, the very words which he had uttered orally when he was present with them. "If I come again I will not spare." ἐὰν ἔλθω εἰς τὸ πάλιν, οὐ φείσομαι: so that, (unless the double resemblance be set aside as entirely accidental), we are met by the fact that a purposed visit which in xiii. 2 is spoken of as a future possibility, is in i. 23 and in ii. 1 treated as an abandoned plan, a purpose of the past, which the writer mentions only in order to explain his reasons for not having carried it out.

It is noteworthy that the translators both of the Authorised and Revised Versions, from not observing the correspondence with the previous announcement, seem to have regarded the οὐκέτι in i. 23 as unintelligible if given the plain meaning "no longer," "no more," "not again," which it always bears, alike in classical and in Biblical Greek.* The translators of the Authorised Version ventured so far as to render it as if it were equivalent to "Not as yet"; which it never is. The editors of the Revised Version were too accomplished scholars to repeat so palpable a mistranslation: yet they seem to have regarded the simple meaning of οὐκέτι as being so utterly inexplicable here, that they have taken refuge in an extraordinary periphrasis "I forbare to come." An English reader would naturally be led to suppose that "I forbare" represented a corresponding verb in the original. No one could possibly conjecture that it was intended to represent the Greek word οὐκέτι.

The third sentence which I shall adduce is to be found, like the first, in the paragraph in which St. Paul is speaking to the Corinthians of the Epistle which he had lately sent to them before their repentance. It occurs only six verses later than the first sentence, *i.e.* in ii. 9, "For to this end also did I write, that I might know the proof of you, whether ye are obedient in all things"; with which I would compare 2nd Corinthians x. 6, "Being in a readiness to avenge all disobedience when your obedience shall be fulfilled." The words of ii. 9 imply that St. Paul, when he wrote them, was satisfied that the Corinthian

---

* Compare Matt. xix. 6; Mark x. 8; Luke xv. 19, 21; John iv. 22; vi. 66; Acts xx. 25, 38; Rom. vi. 9; xiv. 15; 2nd Cor. v. 16; Gal. iii. 25; iv. 7; Eph. ii. 19; Philem. 16; Heb. x. 18, 26.

THE IDENTIFICATION

Church was now obedient in all things; and later on he expressly asserts this; for in viii. 15, 16 he says (speaking of the result of Titus's mission), "Whilst he remembereth the obedience of you all, how with fear and trembling ye received him. I rejoice therefore that I have confidence in you in all things." He is now so far from any longer entertaining the purpose "to avenge disobedience" that he gives the Corinthian Church a *carte blanche* in the matter of forgiveness, in the very next verse to the one which I have quoted as a parallel, "To whom ye forgive anything I forgive also" (ii. 10).

There are two considerations which should be borne in mind in estimating the importance which should be attached to the correspondence of these three pairs of parallel passages. First, that in each of these pairs, the act, or purpose, or feeling, which in the four chapters (x.-xiii.) is present, or future, in the nine Chapters (i-ix.) is spoken of as belonging to the past. And secondly—that these parallel passages have not been obtained by pressing into the service everything which looked like a parallelism in a long Epistle, without regard to the subject-matter of which the writer was treating; but that, on the contrary, one term of each of these pairs has been found in the brief compass of a paragraph of twelve verses (from i. 23 to ii. 10) in which the writer is expressly speaking to the Corinthians of the epistle which he wrote to them out of much affliction and anguish of heart. It should also be observed that while this paragraph occurs in the opening part of the Epistle, two of the corresponding sentences from 2nd Corinthians have been found in the closing Chapter of that epistle. This is what might have been expected, *a priori*, in letters standing to each other in the relation in which I contend that these epistles stand. It would in such a case be highly probable that the opening part of the later letter would contain references to the thoughts and plans of the writer when he was concluding the letter which immediately preceded it, though not necessarily confined to the concluding portion.

In addition to the proofs of identification furnished by these passages, St. Paul has given us an opportunity of applying marks of identification on a larger scale, in the four particulars about the missing epistle which are mentioned in the epistle which he wrote from Macedonia, and which have already been compared with 1st Corinthians. Taking them in the same order, let us compare them with 2nd Corinthians, Chapters x.–xiii.

The first note of identification, (to which it is admitted by all that 1st Corinthians corresponds very imperfectly), is furnished to us by the statement that it was written "out of much affliction, and anguish of heart with many tears."

It will scarcely be denied that the contents of Chapters x.–xiii. are such as we might on *a priori*

THE IDENTIFICATION

grounds have conjectured to have been written under the influence of feelings like these. Not only do we find many passages which we can well believe to have been blotted with tears (as, for instance, xi. 11, 15, 20, 21); but the style and manner of the whole writing present the very characteristics which we should expect to find in a letter written out of much anguish of heart. From the very beginning of Chapter x. to the farewell blessing at the close of Chapter xiii., they correspond, and correspond in a most striking manner with the description given by St. Paul in 3rd Corinthians Chapter ii. 4 of the emotions under the influence of which he had written to the Corinthians a short time before.

The second note of identification is given in 3rd Corinthians Chapters vii. 8, 9, where the writer lets us see that his affliction had been caused by the conduct of the Corinthians, and that he had expressed his sense of this so strongly in the epistle to which he there refers, that after he had sent it to them he for a time repented having done so ("Though I did repent," 3rd Cor. vii. 8).

In 1st Corinthians the blame occupies but a small portion of the letter, which contains also a good deal of praise, and an amount of valuable instruction which far exceeds either; but in 2nd Corinthians x.–xiii. the expressions of displeasure are no longer a small portion of the whole, and they are blended with no praise. The keynote here is "If I come again I will not spare." There is only one other epistle of St. Paul (the Epistle to the Galatians) which shows anything approaching the displeasure which is here apparent throughout.

The third mark may be gathered from 3rd Corinthians iii. 1, where the question "Do we begin *again* to commend ourselves?" implies that the writer has done this on some previous occasion but is not going to do so again; and from v. 12 where he makes a positive assertion that he is not going to repeat it, in which he repeats the word "again" (πάλιν).

When we turn to 2nd Corinthians x.–xiii. the word πάλιν, and the references to self-commendation become full of meaning; for he must be indeed a careless reader who has never been struck by this characteristic in these Chapters. Indeed the writer again and again calls attention to what he is doing. In these four Chapters the word καυχᾶσθαι occurs fifteen times, and the word καύχησις twice,—*i.e.* in xi. 10 and xi. 17. The first of these passages would be especially likely to leave a painful feeling in the minds of the Corinthian Christians even after their reconciliation.

A comparison of the way in which the writer employs these words, and the cognate word καύχημα, in Chapters i.–ix., with his use of them in x.–xiii., reveals a contrast so delicate and so suggestive that, I think, it alone would convince me that he wrote Chapters i.–ix. with recollection of Chapters x.–xiii.,

THE IDENTIFICATION

and with the conviction that his readers recollected them also. The first time that he employs the word καύχησις is in the passage which has been already discussed (i. 12), and he there uses the definite article, and proceeds, as we have seen, to explain what it had really meant: "The boasting is this." Then in the fourteenth verse, with a delicate touch, which is peculiarly characteristic of St. Paul, he brings in the word καύχημα, and gives it a new application "Ye are our boast"; and having given this turn to the word, it is in this way that he employs it and its cognate words henceforth in these Chapters.

Thus in vii. 4 he writes: "Great is my boasting (καύχησις) on your behalf"; in vii. 14 he speaks of having boasted of them to Titus, and in the ninth Chapter of having boasted of them to the Macedonians. There is only one exception, *i.e.* in v. 12, and in that passage he is their boast, as they are his in all the other passages. But he never once reverts to the painful meaning of self-assertion rendered necessary by their depreciation of him, in which sense he so constantly used the word in 2nd Corinthians x.–xiii. I do not think it is possible that this can be merely accidental, but I have never seen it noticed by any commentator; when they allude to the words at all, they speak solely of the number of times that they are used, without taking notice of the remarkable and significant difference of meaning.

These are not the only instances in which St. Paul

gives a similar turn in Chapters i.–ix. to expressions which he had used in x.–xiii. When a word used at the time of their estrangement in a stern and painful sense, is capable of being used in a gracious sense he seems purposely to do this when he writes to the Corinthians after their repentance. Thus the θαρρῶ εἰς ὑμᾶς of x. 1, 2 (confidence against you) is replaced in vii. 16 by θαρρῶ ἐν ὑμῖν (I have confidence in you); and πεποίθησις,* which was similarly used in an unfavourable way in x. 2, is given a favourable meaning in i. 15. When a word is not capable of being thus transformed, and when the idea which it represents cannot be altogether excluded in making some needful explanation, we have seen how he substitutes another word, as "sorrow" for severity ii. 1 "I determined not to come unto you again in sorrow," and in ii. 3 "That when I came I might not have sorrow" instead of "That when I came I might not use severity"; whereas in xiii. 10 the sterner word had been used "That when present I may not use severity."

I have spoken of these last points as if I assumed the priority of Chapters x.–xiii. I was obliged to do so in order to bring out their meaning. Taken in this order of time these contrasts are full of significance and beauty; but they cannot be read in the reverse order. They are like the valves of the veins which

* This point about πεποίθησις was suggested to me by the Rev. F. R. M. Hitchcock.

THE IDENTIFICATION

revealed to Harvey the secret of the circulation of the blood by opening in one direction only.

A fourth mark of identification of the Epistle referred to in Chapter ii. 4 is furnished by i. 23 and ii. 1, which show that the Apostle was at the time when he wrote, contemplating and at the same time shrinking from, the payment of a visit which must be of a severe character, and that in the end, out of mercy to them, he did not pay it.

With this mark we have seen already that the references to St. Paul's intentions in 1st Corinthians xvi. do not correspond at all. On the other hand 2nd Corinthians x.–xiii. corresponds as perfectly with this note of identification as it does with the three previous ones; for 2nd Corinthians xii. 20, 21 and xiii. 1, 2 show that the Apostle was when he wrote these passages contemplating a visit of the very character which the identification requires; and the last-mentioned verse proves in addition the fact that he was hesitating about it. The words "If I come again I will not spare," show that, at the time when they were written, the coming itself was uncertain, but that there seemed to be only too much certainty about the character of the visit, if it were paid then.

That these notes of identification do not form a key which would fit any lock, may be seen from the fact that there is not one of the eleven remaining epistles of St. Paul which would answer to any one of them, except the Epistle to the Galatians, and that it would not answer to the last-mentioned mark.

If these proofs are valid, it follows of necessity that Chapters x.–xiii. must have been written, not from Macedonia, as were Chapters i.–ix., but from Ephesus: and this consequence of the theory lays it open either to refutation or confirmation if it be found to contain any descriptive phrase indicating the geographical position of the writer. It does contain such a phrase.* In x. 16 the Apostle speaks of preaching "the Gospel even unto the lands on the other side of you," εἰς τὰ ὑπερέκεινα ὑμῶν where the addition of ὑμῶν seems intended to define the locality of these lands as being on the other side of Corinth. Now a straight line drawn from Macedonia to Achaia would, if produced, not touch land till it reached the coast of Africa; whereas a straight line drawn from Ephesus to Corinth would be continued through Italy and Spain, the very lands which, as we learn from the Epistle to the Romans, St. Paul was planning to visit. I feel certain that if it were the received theory which placed the writer of this sentence at Ephesus, the coincidence would have been noticed by every commentator, and it would have been regarded as a fatal objection to any new theory if

Chaps. x.–xiii. not written from Macedonia.

---

* This has been noticed by Professor Hausrath in his pamphlet *Der Vier-Capitel-Brief des Paulus an die Korinther.* Heidelberg, 1870.

THE IDENTIFICATION

it necessitated a change which would deprive this phrase of any part of its point and force. A new theory of course requires far more proof than would be thought sufficient for an old one; but it is an indication that we are on the right track when a conclusion to which we have been led on altogether different grounds, gives to a geographical expression an appropriateness which it has never had for any readers since that day, now more than eighteen hundred years ago, when this epistle was read for the last time in the original manuscript by some member of the Corinthian Church.

If Chapters x.–xiii. appeared in our Bibles, in the same order as they do now, but as a separate Epistle, I think that it would be generally admitted that the marks of identification which have been adduced would justify the conclusion that that Epistle was the same, or part of the same, Epistle which is referred to in Chapter ii. 4; and that we had no need and no right to resort to the hypothesis of a lost epistle, when we were in possession of a document which corresponded in so many and so remarkable particulars with the description given by the Author himself. The rule *entia non sunt multiplicanda praeter necessitatem* would in that case be applicable. But as it is, it will no doubt be objected that these Chapters are not an *ens;* but have come down to us as part of the very epistle that contains the description to which they

94 SECOND AND THIRD CORINTHIANS

appear to correspond. We have now to test the conclusiveness of the reply by an examination of the document in question.

THE COMPOSITE NATURE OF THE DOCUMENT WHICH APPEARS IN THE CANON AS SECOND CORINTHIANS

The occasion of St. Paul's writing Chapters i.-ix. was the successful result of the mission of Titus and of a letter which the Apostle had himself written. This is admitted by all. The keynote of these Chapters is truly described in the *Speaker's Commentary* as "Comfort in affliction"; the word παράκλησις occurring eleven times in these nine Chapters. St. Paul does not leave us in doubt as to the cause of this comfort and of the joy with which he now overflows (vii. 4). It was the coming of Titus, and not his coming only, but the tidings which he brought with him of the repentance and zeal of the Corinthian Church, which had changed his great sorrow into great joy. This keynote of παράκλησις is struck in the very beginning of the first Chapter and it is maintained to the close of the ninth. Whenever the writer digresses in order to give counsel or warning he comes back again to the subject of his thankfulness and joy, and the completeness of the

COMPOSITE NATURE OF DOCUMENT 95

reconciliation which has been effected; and at the end of the seventh Chapter he concludes the subjects which he has been discussing with the words "I rejoice, therefore, that I have confidence in you in all things."

The two following Chapters deal with the question of the collection, and in them the same affectionate and cheerful tone is maintained. The writer's approaching visit to Corinth seems to be looked forward to with pleasure, the only cause of apprehension being lest, as he has been praising the Corinthian Church so highly to the Macedonians, they may not in that one particular be found to be quite so good as he has depicted them; this apprehension being expressed in language which is affectionate and almost playful. "Lest we (that we say not, ye) should be ashamed in this same confident boasting." He closes these Chapters with the ejaculation "Thanks be unto God for his unspeakable gift."

Then, after this climax of adoring gratitude, without the least explanation, all is suddenly changed, and a torrent of mingled pathos and indignation is poured out, being continued through four Chapters till the final farewell and blessing of the last four verses; the cheerful tone being never resumed for a moment. These four verses indeed express earnest affection, but I cannot agree with Weber that there is in this anything inconsistent with the argument of the four Chapters at the close of which they stand;

for these four Chapters are, after all, the utterances of love, though it be wounded love. We need not therefore think it strange if the Apostle, before he closes his letter, allows the expression of his love to predominate in the four verses in which he bids farewell to those who were so dear to him. Even in the severe Epistle to the Galatians the last word before the final amen is "Brothers" ἀδελφοί, and the last sentence is a blessing. There is, however, at the close of these four Chapters no return to the attitude of joy and thankfulness with which Chapters i.–ix. both began and ended.

If, seeking for a clue to guide us through these difficulties, we scrutinise the first sentence where this change makes its appearance, we not only find no reason or explanation furnished by the writer, but are further confronted with the strange fact that the second word of this sentence is the conjunction δέ, seeming to connect the sentence with something which has gone before, and that the passage has all the appearance of being the continuation of an argument homogeneous with itself; for, in addition to the fact that it begins with a conjunction, it contains an allusion to an objection which had been brought against the Apostle, which it brings before us not as if the subject were now for the first time introduced, but as if it had been already mentioned. Furthermore, St. Paul in this opening sentence accosts those to whom his reproaches are addressed simply as

COMPOSITE NATURE OF DOCUMENT

"ye," without any addition or qualification to show that he is no longer addressing the Church at large, or the repentant majority, but an unrepentant minority, who have dissociated themselves from the submission of their fellow Churchmen.

Prof. Hausrath in his treatise, *Der Vier-Capitel-Brief*, puts forward a curious hypothesis about this sentence. According to him the clue is to be found in the word αὐτός, which denotes that what follows belongs to the Apostle in a sense in which that which preceded it did not. He conjectures that these four Chapters were probably an appendix to an epistle written by the brethren at Ephesus in support of St. Paul, and that the name of Aquila may have been the most prominent in it, as he would be likely to have special influence, having helped to found the Corinthian Church.

Prof. Hausrath might have found in the Epistle to the Galatians phrases not unlike that which he regards as so significant, especially "'Ἰδὲ ἐγὼ Παῦλος λέγω ὑμῖν" in Galatians v. 2, where, instead of pointing a contrast with something preceding it, which had not been said by St. Paul, the expression continues with added emphasis a connected argument. This is the function which, as I think, was discharged by the phrase αὐτὸς δὲ ἐγὼ Παῦλος as it stood in the original manuscript which was written at St. Paul's dictation; for my conjecture is that the destruction by some accident of the earlier part of the manuscript has broken off the connection at a point which is now the beginning of the tenth Chapter, but which appears to have been originally the middle of an impassioned argument or appeal. Αὐτός would seem to be used in connection with the taunts to which the Apostle was referring in the discourse of which we have now only the latter portion. "I myself who am thus depreciated by you."

Klöpper, in his commentary, quotes Hausrath's surmise with glee, exclaiming triumphantly that the father of the theory of the four-Chaptered Epistle has dug its grave with his own hands. Klöpper is, I think, a little hasty in jumping to the conclusion that the theory which he defends is the only alternative to this conjecture of Hausrath.

It is not so much in the employment of the word αὐτός as in that of the conjunction δέ that, in my opinion, the true clue is to be found. δέ, as Winer teaches, connects while it opposes, whereas ἀλλά expresses proper and sharp opposition. δέ is indeed frequently used by St. Paul almost as an equivalent to "and."[*] But, at the beginning of Chapter x. even ἀλλά would be utterly inadequate to express the sharpness of the opposition between the contents of that Chapter and the ejaculation, "Thanks be unto God for his unspeakable gift," with which Chapter ix. so appropriately concluded.

[*] Professor Mahaffy informs me that the same use is found in all the Papyrus Greek of this time.

THE MAJORITY AND MINORITY

The startling abruptness of the transition at this point is to some extent concealed from ordinary readers by the division into Chapters; but all commentators have noticed it, and have felt the necessity for some explanation. The explanation generally adopted is that the tidings brought by Titus were not altogether favourable. All who were well disposed had been humbled by the Apostle's rebukes; but his adversaries had been further embittered. The first nine Chapters of 2nd Corinthians are accordingly supposed to be addressed to the repentant majority, and the four concluding chapters to the rebellious minority.

An objection to this theory which at once suggests itself is that where St. Paul is supposed to turn to the rebellious minority, he addresses them simply as "you," as if they were the same persons whom he had been addressing all along. Indeed the only appearance of a distinction which he makes is not between them and a majority better than themselves, but rather between them and a still more rebellious minority. "I beseech you, that I may not, when present, shew courage with the confidence wherewith I count to be bold against some, which count of us as if we walked according to the flesh."

But beside this objection, the description which St. Paul gives in Chapters i.-ix. of the manner in which his letter was received, plainly describes a state of feeling so universal and so strong as to be inconsistent with the existence of such an openly rebellious minority as would be required to account for the language of x.–xiii. He speaks of the Corinthians as having received Titus "with fear and trembling" (vii. 15); he records how Titus "told us your earnest desire, your mourning, your fervent mind toward me" (vii. 7); and he adds, "For behold this self-same thing that ye sorrowed after a godly sort, what carefulness it wrought in you, yea, what clearing of yourselves, yea, what indignation, yea, what fear, yea, what vehement desire, yea, what zeal, yea, what revenge; In all things ye have approved yourselves to be clear in the matter." And at the close of the seventh chapter he twice emphatically speaks of the *universality* of this movement of zeal and Godly fear. In vii. 13 he says, "His spirit was refreshed by you all." Again, in the fifteenth verse, "Whilst he remembereth the obedience of you *all*, how with fear and trembling ye received him." Even the chief offender himself was not only overwhelmed by the force of public opinion within the Church, but was also moved to true repentance, so that the Apostle was satisfied that his case no longer called for punishment, but rather for forgiveness and reconciliation.

Professor Klöpper (whose commentary on 2nd Corinthians is referred to by eminent English commentators as conclusively establishing its unity) finds himself so hard pressed by some of these passages that he has recourse to a summary method of disposing of them by describing them as "idealistic" and "to be taken *cum grano salis*." His adoption of this heroic method of exposition is a tribute to the strength of the proof which St. Paul's language furnishes if we allow him only to speak.

But—it will be said—St. Paul does undoubtedly speak of a majority in Chapter ii. 6, and this implies that there was a minority, which must have been composed of persons who were opposed to the majority on this point.

I fully agree that this is the obvious meaning of his language; and I believe that the facts which his reference to this circumstance discloses, and the way in which he deals with them, give us a glimpse of an incident in early Church History (which would otherwise have escaped us), and of the great Apostle's treatment of a situation of some delicacy. But if we wish to gain all the information which this passage is capable of furnishing, we must come to it without prejudice, and endeavour to ascertain from it what the real character of the minority was, instead of settling beforehand what it must have been. I think the interpretation of these verses has suffered from having been mixed up with the question of Chapters x.-xiii. The result of this has been that critics have approached it with a keen desire to find in the mention of a majority some explanation of the severity of those Chapters; so that they have at once jumped to the conclusion that the minority must have been composed of mischievous and evil-disposed persons, who had resisted the punishment of the offender, and still refused to acknowledge its justice. The eminent commentator, Meyer, for instance, thus comments upon the passage. "To the minority there may have belonged—partly the most lax in morality, and partly also opponents of the Apostle, the latter resisting on principle."

If, instead of prejudging the question, we seek to ascertain the character of the Minority by interrogating the passage in which the Majority is spoken of, we are confronted with the fact that St. Paul devotes himself altogether to defending the adequacy (ἱκανόν) of the sentence, and says nothing about its justice; nor is there a single word in the paragraph which either asserts or implies that its justice had been disputed by anyone. We may next notice that he is addressing certain persons in the second person as "you" (ὑμᾶς), and that he appears to distinguish them from the Majority; for he speaks to them of the majority in the third person, and defends the adequacy of their sentence. This, even if we had no further guidance, would make it probable that the Minority are addressed here, and that they were composed of ultra-Paulinists, or, at any rate, of members of the Church of Corinth who were dissatisfied with the punishment inflicted by the

The Character of the Minority.

CHARACTER OF THE MINORITY 103

Majority, because, in their opinion, it was too light.

But this probability is converted into certainty by the phrase τοὐναντίον, which immediately follows. The words "You should on the contrary forgive him" would have had no meaning if those who were being thus exhorted were not pursuing or proposing to pursue a contrary course; and the contrary of forgiveness is the refusal to forgive, the demand for further punishment.

If we would understand aright St. Paul's attitude towards this minority, we must not fail further to notice the sensitive care with which he avoids saying a single word of censure beyond what was absolutely necessary to dissuade them from their purpose. He says "contrariwise" but he does not complete the sentence by adding "contrariwise to what you propose." He does not even say "You *ought* to forgive" but "It is for you to forgive." He evidently felt that their demand for severity sprang from their loyalty and affection, and not from any evil or corrupt motive.

Yet—partly for that very reason—the situation was a delicate and critical one. If the Apostle had encouraged the complaint of the Minority, and declared the decision of the majority to be inadequate, he might have given the Corinthians the impression that he regarded the Minority as his only true friends, and might thus have revived the baneful party spirit which had been the germ from which such terrible evil had so lately developed. He did not wish that the reconciliation in which he so greatly rejoiced should be marred, as was David's return to his kingdom, when the boast of the men of Judah about the king's nearer kinship to themselves, changed the loyal enthusiasm of the Israelites into jealousy and ill-will. St. Paul was resolved that Satan should not thus get an advantage over them.

But the Apostle had also another reason for his decision. He was convinced that the offender was sincerely and deeply repentant, and he believed him to be in danger of being overwhelmed by the pangs of remorse. It is a very significant circumstance that, believing this, he seems to have looked specially to the members of the Minority (by the expression of their full forgiveness to the penitent) to prevent him from being swallowed up by excess of sorrow. It is to them that he appeals in the sixth and seventh verses; and he does not seem merely to apprehend that the penitent would be crushed if a further punishment were inflicted by the vote of the community—the Majority were able to prevent that—but rather that he may be crushed in spirit unless the very persons to whom St. Paul is now appealing, pursue a course directly contrary to that which they had chosen; unless they forgive, and comfort him, and confirm their love towards him. It would appear that the Apostle must have received

CHARACTER OF THE MINORITY

information which convinced him that the man in the bitterness of his repentance did not take comfort from the fact that the Majority looked upon his offence as sufficiently punished. *They* might forgive him, but he did not forgive himself, and could not be brought to do so unless those whom he regarded as the special friends of the Apostle ceased to frown on him, and confirmed their love toward him.*

These zealous adherents of St. Paul, whom he thought worthy of being treated with so great tenderness, and to whose moral influence he attached so much importance, have, I maintain, been grievously maligned by modern commentators.

---

* It is generally assumed that this offender is to be identified with the incestuous person who is mentioned in 1st Corinthians. I shall confine myself to stating some reasons which have led me to look on this identification as being at least very doubtful. Is it probable that St. Paul, who always speaks so solemnly of the enormity of offences against purity, would have said that he had written of so terrible a moral offence as that of the committer of incest, merely that the Corinthians' care for himself in the sight of God might appear? "I wrote not for his cause that did the wrong, nor for his cause that suffered the wrong, but that your earnest care for us might be made manifest in the sight of God" (vii. 12). It would not be any great proof either of their obedience to St. Paul or of their care for him in the sight of God, that they had condemned an abomination which even without the light of Christianity, the law written in the hearts of men led many to condemn. In 1st Corinthians he seems expressly to declare that he *has* written about the case of incest "for his sake that did the wrong," *i.e.* that his spirit might be saved in the day of the Lord Jesus. It appears more likely that the offence mentioned in 3rd Corinthians was of an altogether different kind, but what it was we can never know with certainty, owing to the loss of the first part of 2nd Corinthians.

They have been transformed into a party of obstinate rebels, whose opposition to the Apostle was only inflamed by the submission of their fellow Churchmen. Even when some critics have been struck by the fact of the mention of the adequacy of the sentence, and have thereby been constrained to admit that the Minority must have advocated a severer one, the remark is invariably added that they must have done this from malignant and treacherous motives, wishing to entrap the Apostle into an act of severity, and then to use this as a means of undermining his influence. They have actually been identified with Satan, and it has been supposed that it is their devices which are referred to in the eleventh verse. I believe that when St. Paul in that passage spoke of Satan, he meant Satan, and not any member of the Church, either of the Minority or Majority. Satan he regarded as the author of strife and ill-will; and, as he recalled the events of the last twelve months, whose painful history had, as it were, been burned into his memory; as he recollected the startling rapidity with which the party spirit noticed in 1st Corinthians had developed into the strife, jealousy, wraths, factions, backbitings, whisperings, swellings, tumults spoken of in 2nd Corinthians; it is not surprising that he should have exclaimed, "We are not ignorant of his devices."

I think that any appearance of obscurity, which

CHARACTER OF THE MINORITY 107

later readers may find in this passage, has arisen from St. Paul's desire to give as little recognition as he possibly could to the division of the Church of Corinth into parties, as well as from his anxiety not to wound the feelings of the Minority whose proposal he was setting aside. He must necessarily have received some communication on the subject to which he here refers — either by a verbal communication through Titus or in a letter or letters brought by him. As the difference of opinion had been sufficient to require a vote of some kind to be taken, and as the community at Corinth had already, (as we have seen), adopted the plan of writing letters to St. Paul; it is not at all improbable that he received from both parties communications in which they gave their reasons for the course which they had adopted. If to these communications the Apostle had written separate replies, this course would have involved a recognition of the Corinthian parties; and it would have had the further inconvenience that the reply intended for one party would sooner or later be certain to come into the hands of members of the opposite party. To warn them against this would have been useless, and would also have been absolutely inconsistent with his condemnation of divisions in the Church. The only alternative, then, was to touch on the matter in the letter written to the whole Church. This he does as briefly as possible, yet in a manner which would make his meaning quite clear to those whom he wished to influence. It is not improbable that the Minority had complained of having been outvoted by the Majority and that the words ἡ ἐπιτιμία αὕτη ἡ ὑπὸ τῶν πλειόνων referred to some passage in their letter. At any rate, the reference must have been perfectly intelligible to them. But St. Paul makes this appeal to a section as brief as possible, and he takes the greatest pains to show that in the remainder of his letter he is addressing the whole community and that his praise is intended for all. It can scarcely be an accidental circumstance that immediately before turning for a moment to a section, he declared that the offence had grieved them *all;* and in his praise of their obedience he afterwards twice repeats and emphasises this word "all." In vii. 13 he is not content with saying "Titus's spirit was refreshed by you" but adds "by you *all,*" ἀπὸ πάντων ὑμῶν, and in the fifteenth verse of the same Chapter he described Titus as "remembering the obedience of you all," πάντων ὑμῶν. This emphatic repetition of the word "all" seems to show that the writer intended to make it clear that he was not the Apostle of a party, but of the whole Church of Corinth, and that he was anxious that every member—alike of the Majority and Minority—should feel that he had a share in St. Paul's commendation.

The attempt, then, to explain the severity of

CHARACTER OF THE MINORITY

Chapters x.-xiii. by the hypothesis of the existence of an openly rebellious minority in the Church of Corinth breaks down in two ways: firstly, because the language used about the universality as well as enthusiasm of the submission made by the Corinthian Christians, at the time of Titus's visit, leaves us no room for the existence of such an openly rebellious minority as is required; and secondly because St. Paul plainly indicates to us the real character of the minority by the words which he addresses to them, and shows that character to be the very reverse of what it has been supposed to be.

But these are not the only difficulties which beset this hypothesis. While the description of the repentance of the Corinthian Church given in Chapters i.-ix., seems to leave no room for an openly rebellious minority, the language of Chapters x.-xiii. leaves no room for a repentant majority. The rebels are from first to last addressed, not as a section of the Church, but as the Church of Corinth itself.

Thus in xi. 8 the Apostle says, "I robbed *other* Churches," implying by his words that it is a Church that he is addressing; and in xii. 13 he says, "In what were ye inferior to other Churches?" In Chapters i.-ix. St. Paul interrupts his exhortations to assure his readers that he does not write to condemn them, and he shows in different places in these Chapters a keen anxiety that nothing may revive the painful feelings of the past. If Chapters x.–xiii. were part of the same letter addressed to an unrepentant minority whose rebellious spirit was in sharp contrast to that of the repentant majority, it is inconceivable that the Apostle should never once from beginning to end of these four Chapters have written a single sentence to assure the Majority that his reproaches were not intended for them, but only for the rebellious section. Instead of doing this, he again and again uses language the plain meaning of which would seem to include the whole community. For instance, in xi. 10: "As the truth of Christ is in me, no man shall stop me of this boasting in the regions of Achaia"; and in xiii. 2 he expressly includes all, in language which it seems impossible to mistake, "Being absent now I write to them which heretofore have sinned and to all the rest, that if I come again I will not spare." Even if the Apostle had not used the unmistakable words, τοῖς λοιποῖς πᾶσιν, the mere fact that he was here referring back to a threat uttered when his relations with the community were evidently greatly strained, and that he now expressly declared that his present warning was a repetition of that threat, would almost of necessity give to the second threat as wide an application as had been given to the first.

Some commentators of eminence have employed

THE HYPOTHESIS OF LATER NEWS

another hypothesis to explain the divergence between Chapters i.-ix. and x.-xiii. They have supposed that when St. Paul had written as far as to the end of the ninth Chapter fresh news arrived, this time of a distinctly unfavourable character, and that the four Chapters which close the Epistle, as we have it, were written in consequence of the receipt of this information. *[The Hypothesis of later News.]*

If this hypothesis be true, and if we are to take 1st Corinthians as indicating by its tone the gravity of the situation when the Apostle wrote with many tears out of much affliction and anguish of heart at the time of the mission of Titus, and 2nd Corinthians x.-xiii. as indicating the gravity of the situation which arose in consequence of this new development, then must these later tidings have caused the complete destruction of all the hopes which had been excited by the result of Titus's mission, and showed the state of things at Corinth to be worse than ever. For the tone of 2nd Corinthians x.-xiii. is beyond all comparison more sorrowful and more indignant than that of 1st Corinthians. Is it possible that, if news so momentous had arrived, St. Paul should never have mentioned it, never alluded to it in any way; that he should have sent to the rebellious Church the praise of them which he had already written, adding on the blame without explanation, joining the blame to the praise by the conjunction δέ, and (strangest of all) falling back on a declaration* which he had made before the mission of Titus, as if nothing had happened in the meantime? Klöpper admits that it is surprising (auffallend) that the writer should say nothing of any unfavourable news, and should instead go back to the threat which he had uttered during his second visit to Corinth. For "surprising" I would substitute "incredible." The fact that 2nd Corinthians xiii. 2 thus goes back to the time of the visit is a strong proof that, when it was written, there could not have intervened any change in the situation of such critical importance as that which had been brought about (as St. Paul shows us in i.-ix.) by Titus's mission and by the letter of the Apostle. I am convinced that the true way of escape from this difficulty is to assign to Chapters x.-xiii. a date earlier than that of the mission of Titus.

Another way has, however, been suggested by a German theologian named Drescher, writing in the number of *Studien und Kritiken* for January 1897. Instead of dating 2nd Corinthians xiii. 2 before Titus's mission, he seeks to place the visit to which it refers after that mission, and thus assigns to Chapters x.-xiii. a date later than Chapters i.-ix. While this view is, of course, opposed to the view of Klöpper with regard to the unity of 2nd Corinthians, it agrees with him in what I

* Ch. xiii. 2.

THE HYPOTHESIS OF LATER NEWS 113

believe to be a much more important matter; *i.e.* in holding that Titus made an incorrect diagnosis of the situation at Corinth, and misled St. Paul, so that the nine Chapters were written under the influence of an illusion. He quotes with warm approval Klöpper's remarks on this point; and gives it as his opinion that St. Paul's choleric temperament was easily carried away, by excessive and exaggerated alternations of hope and fear, so that he formed an opinion of the state of things from the report of Titus which he afterwards found to be false. The theory of Titus's mistake and St. Paul's illusion, which is so uncompromisingly put forward by this writer, is also the logical result of the hypothesis of the arrival of fresh news of a contradictory character before the letter was finished. If Titus's account of the repentance of the Corinthian Church, as it is given to us by St. Paul, be correct, it would be impossible, unless some new subject of dispute had been introduced, that the old causes of bitterness could have so soon revived, and in so acute a form; and it is the old causes of bitterness, very much intensified but without any new element, which we find in Chapters x.-xiii.

Another hypothesis intended to explain the divergence between Chapters i.-ix. and x.-xiii. has been suggested by a learned, able, and ingenious scholar, the Rev. Newport White, in a reply which he published in the *Expositor* to two articles of mine which had appeared in the same periodical on this subject. His explanation is that "the same persons are addressed but from totally different points of view, the motive of the first part of the letter being the repentance of the Corinthians for their immorality and profanity, the theme of the second being the increased encouragement which at the same time they were giving to the party who depreciated the apostolic character of St. Paul."

Mr. White has not quoted any passages from these nine Chapters in support of his theory; and, as a matter of fact, there is not a single passage in the praise, of which they are so full, which makes express mention of their previous immorality and profanity. The prominent subject is their acknowledgment of St. Paul, whose messenger they received with fear and trembling. But this is the very topic which if Mr. White's theory were true should be conspicuous by its absence. I think that the theory must rest on the assumption that the offender, mentioned in the second and seventh of these Chapters, is to be identified with the incestuous person whose case is mentioned in 1st Corinthians. If this be so, it is rather unfortunate for the theory that St. Paul in the seventh Chapter expressly says that his only reason for referring to the case of this offender (whoever he was) was the bearing of his case on the relation of the Corinthian Church to

THE VISITS OF TITUS TO CORINTH

himself. "I wrote not for his cause that did the wrong, nor for his cause that suffered wrong, but that your earnest care for us might be made manifest unto you in the sight of God." In Chapters x.–xiii. the same subject is prominent amid its blame, which is prominent in the praise of i.–ix.; but there is one passage which Mr. White evidently feels to be a difficulty for his hypothesis. I refer to xii. 21 where St. Paul says "Lest, when I come again, my God will humble me among you, and I should mourn for many that have sinned heretofore, and repented not of the uncleanness and fornication and lasciviousness which they committed."

Mr. White's comment on this passage is "After all their seeming repentance, and his acceptance of it, it might well be that disloyalty and impurity went hand in hand." After this admission it is somewhat difficult to see how much of the theory is left, or to comprehend what it was for which St. Paul so warmly praised them in i.–ix., if "disloyalty and impurity" were going "hand in hand" among them.

THE VISITS OF TITUS TO CORINTH

The subject of the visits which were paid by Titus to Corinth is one which is of capital importance in this enquiry. Two such visits are spoken of in Chapters i.–ix. The first being that from which he returned to St. Paul with tidings of the repentance and renewed loyalty of the Corinthian Church; and the second the visit on which he had just been sent in order to forward the business of the collection at Corinth.

In Chapters x.–xiii. there is also reference made to a visit of Titus to Corinth, *i.e.* in xii. 18. "I summoned Titus, and with him I sent a brother. Did Titus make a gain of you? Walked we not by the same Spirit? walked we not in the same steps?"

Two opinions about these visits are held generally by commentators on these Epistles. First, that the visit mentioned in xii. 18 is to be identified with one or other of those spoken of in Chapters i.–ix.; secondly, that Titus had been accused of dishonesty, and that St. Paul is defending him from this charge when he asks, "Did Titus make a gain of you?"

While critics agree in these general principles, they differ as to the visit with which the visit of Chapter xii. 18 is to be identified.

Meyer says that the majority of commentators identify it with the latter of the visits, *i.e.* that mentioned in viii. 6; but he objects that Titus had only started on this second mission; so that St. Paul could not ask, "Did Titus make a gain of you?" in reference to a visit which had yet to be paid.

Jülicher on the other hand, who identifies it with this latter visit, brings against the other view the objection that, if Titus had been accused of pecula-

THE VISITS OF TITUS TO CORINTH

tion during the first visit, St. Paul would not have chosen him to arrange the matter of the Collection in a second visit. This argument against the opposite view seems very strong; but I cannot attach much weight to a positive argument which Jülicher advances in favour of his own view — viz. that the word παρακαλέσαι occurs in viii. 6, and that παρεκάλεσα is found in xii. 18. We must remember that St. Paul had persons who "waited on him continually," and were employed as messengers to the Churches. Under such conditions phrases such as the above would become almost technical, being in constant use; so that the occurrence of one of them twice is a very insufficient mark of identification.

But beside the objections which lie against these views taken separately, there is a further objection to which they are both exposed, but which does not seem to have occurred to their advocates. These identifications are necessarily connected with the theory that xii. 18 was written after the missions with which it is identified; and (as a necessary corollary from this) that St. Paul in xii. 18 is writing to persons whom the first of these visits had stirred into more bitter opposition than before.

To have asked the question "Did Titus make a gain of you?" of persons who had been already irritated by his mission, would have been worse than useless, and would probably have led to the retort "If he did not do so, it was because we were on our guard against him. He tried to deceive us with fair speeches; but he failed." Nor is it easy to see how Titus's abstention from making a gain of the Corinthians during a short embassy when he was sent to bring them to submission, could be regarded as a proof of his honesty. To have attempted it at such a moment would have been an act of folly so short-sighted that abstention from it would not prove sterling honesty, but only common prudence; which would lead even a designing knave first to catch them with guile, in the hope that he might afterwards make a gain of them, when their suspicions had been laid aside.

Amid these difficulties and conflicting views the most legitimate and most hopeful way of seeking to solve the problem is by a careful examination of the whole paragraph.

We must begin as far back as the twelfth verse where St. Paul speaks of his work among his converts during his first visit, and of his having refrained from receiving any contributions from them for his own support. This abstinence had been his practice on both his visits; but, of course, the chief proof of his disinterestedness lay in his not having sought any help from his converts during the two years when he had laboured among them, and they had confided in him. He is thus appealing to the memory of earlier and happier days, and he evidently feels that his readers must go with him so far. The next objection is

THE VISITS OF TITUS TO CORINTH 119

stated in a way which implies that they have done this. "But be it so, I did not myself burden you; but, being crafty, I caught you with guile." This objection he meets by asking the question, "Did I take advantage of you by any one of them whom I have sent unto you?" The form of the question shows that he confidently expects the answer, "No"; that he feels certain that they must admit that those whom he sent to continue the work which he had begun, followed the same disinterested course which he had followed. In the next verse he singles out, and mentions by name, one of those whom he had thus sent; and asks "Did Titus make a gain of you?" He evidently asks this with at least as much confidence as that with which he had asked the former question. He feels that he is driving his accusers from point to point, and the $o\dot{v}$ of the next sentence shows that he is certain that they have already given the answer he wishes. "Walked we not," he triumphantly exclaims, "by the same Spirit? Walked we not in the same steps?"

The whole context shows that it is to some early missionary work of Titus among them that he is referring; and that Titus's name is singled out by him from all those whom he had sent to continue his pastoral work, not because he had been ever accused by the Corinthians, but because he was the last man whom they would have thought of accusing. In mentioning him St. Paul is not touching on a new accusation against another person, the introduction of which here would have interrupted and embarrassed the progress of his argument, but he is giving an effective answer to the original objection which he has been driving back from point to point. I believe, therefore, that the only connection which this passage has with the missions which are spoken of in the Epistle which was written from Macedonia, is to be found in the fact that the same confidence in Titus's influence and popularity which led St. Paul to single him out here from all his fellow-workers, decided him to send him as his ambassador on the difficult mission which we know that he so successfully discharged.

The nature of the mission which is referred to in Chapter xii. 18 is not the only question about the visits of Titus on which I feel constrained to differ from the popular view. There appears to be a consensus of opinion among commentators in favour of the assumption that Titus, when sent to bring the Corinthians to submission, was at the same time enjoined to urge them to contribute to the collection for the poor saints at Jerusalem ; and I believe that this assumption has caused the seventh verse of the eighth Chapter to be mistranslated in a manner which seriously affects its meaning. In that verse the translators of the Revised Version have followed the Authorised Version in the insertion of the word "see." "*See* that ye abound in this grace also."

THE VISITS OF TITUS TO CORINTH

They thus change the verse into a command. They have no precedent in the New Testament to support this interpolation. St. Paul, as well as the other sacred writers, invariably supplies the verb ὁρᾶτε or βλέπετε himself, and does not leave it to his translators to do it for him. Nor is there any precedent in the Septuagint, nor, as I believe, in classical Greek. Alford, indeed, attempts to establish one, quoting the hundred and fifty-sixth line of the *Œdipus Coloneus* ἀλλ' ἵνα τῷδ' ἐν ἀφθέγκτῳ. But the best commentators point out an antecedent for ἵνα a little further down, in the hundred and sixty-second line μετάσταθ', ἀπόβαθι * and do not so much as mention Alford's interpretation.

In the passage which Alford has adduced, the true antecedent appears to have escaped his notice, being out of the proper place of an antecedent, following the ἵνα at a considerable interval, instead of preceding it. But in the passage which we are considering there is not even this excuse for making any interpolation.

* The passage is as follows:—

ἀλλ' ἵνα τῷδ' ἐν ἀ-
φθέγκτῳ μὴ προπέσῃς νάπει
ποιάεντι κάθυδρος οὗ
κρατὴρ μειλιχίων ποτῶν
ῥεύματι συντρέχει,
τῶν, ξένε πάμμορ', εὖ φύλαξαι
μετάσταθ' ἀπόβαθι.

Which Jebb thus translates. "But, lest thy rash steps intrude on the sward of yonder voiceless glade, (be thou well ware of such trespass, unhappy stranger) retire, withdraw."

The author has supplied us with an antecedent in the preceding verse, and has actually taken pains to furnish us with what may fairly be described as verbal finger-posts to direct our attention to it, by so constructing the sixth and seventh verses, that there is a threefold parallelism between them. We have ὥσπερ in the seventh verse answering to καθώς in the sixth; ἵνα answering to ἵνα; and in the seventh verse we have καὶ ἐν ταύτῃ τῇ χάριτι answering to καὶ τὴν χάριν ταύτην in the sixth, showing that the ἵνα of the seventh verse is to be connected with the same antecedent as the ἵνα of the sixth, and that they both refer to the purpose of Titus's second visit. The ἀλλά need not cause us any difficulty; for it is employed a little earlier in this very Epistle (i. 9) to express an ascensive transition, or gradation, and is there correctly translated by "yea" in the Revised Version. If we adopt this rendering here the two verses will yield a clear and connected sense. "I summoned Titus, that as he had made a beginning, so he might accomplish in you this grace also; yea that, as ye abound in everything, in faith, and utterance, and in all diligence, and in your love towards us, so ye may abound in this grace also." The seventh verse appears to have been added by St. Paul in order to avoid any appearance of depreciating the work which Titus had already accomplished among the Corinthian Christians, by the description of it in the sixth verse as a beginning. The seventh verse

THE VISITS OF TITUS TO CORINTH

shows how much was included in that $\pi\rho o\epsilon\nu\acute{\eta}\rho\xi\alpha\tau o$; substituting for it the enumeration of the graces which had already been accomplished in them.

The parallelism of the verses shows not only that the $\acute{\iota}\nu\alpha$ of the seventh must have the same antecedent as the $\acute{\iota}\nu\alpha$ of the sixth; but also that $\tau\alpha\acute{\upsilon}\tau\eta\nu$ in the sixth, must have the same force as $\tau\alpha\acute{\upsilon}\tau\eta$ in the seventh.

This is strenuously denied by Alford. He admits that $\tau\alpha\acute{\upsilon}\tau\eta$ in the seventh verse must be taken to be emphatic; but warns his readers against making $\tau\alpha\acute{\upsilon}\tau\eta\nu$ emphatic in the sixth; insisting that the $\kappa\alpha\acute{\iota}$ does not belong to it there, and that it does not mean "this grace also as well as other graces"; though he acknowledges that in the seventh verse the $\kappa\alpha\acute{\iota}$ does belong to the $\tau\alpha\acute{\upsilon}\tau\eta$ and that the two words are to be interpreted in the very way which he forbids in the sixth verse.

The reason for this anxiety to break the connection between the two verses, and to establish a distinction between them, is obvious. Translators and commentators who believed that 1st Corinthians was the epistle which Titus was sent to explain and enforce in the earlier of the two visits spoken of here could not regard any interpretation as admissible which would show that the furtherance of the collection for Jerusalem was the purpose of the later visit only, and formed no part of Titus's commission in the earlier visit.

When, however, we are no longer tied to this assumption, we may ask the question, Is there any antecedent improbability that there was this distinction between the purpose of the two visits, which St. Paul appears to mark for us, when we allow him to speak for himself? I believe that there is no such improbability. It is rather the contrary supposition which is unlikely. Is it probable that the Apostle, who was so jealous of his own independence, that he would not accept assistance even from loyal Churches which reverenced him as their founder and apostle, would when he was sending an ambassador to bring rebels to repentance, commission him at the same time to obtain money contributions towards an object, which, though not connected with St. Paul's material wants, was nevertheless known to be one of his favourite projects, and likely to increase his influence in the mother Church of Christendom? Such a course would have been as inconsistent with wise diplomacy as with the self-respect which formed so marked a feature in St. Paul's character. Prudence would suggest in such a crisis to attempt one thing at a time, and not to mix up objects so incongruous as reducing a rebellious Church to obedience, and asking it for money. But, apart altogether from considerations of diplomacy, I believe that St. Paul would have died before he condescended thus to sue to rebels for what might be represented as a favour to himself. Nor is the passage before us the only one

THE VISITS OF TITUS TO CORINTH

in his writings which shows that his methods in an emergency of this kind were very different from those which have been attributed to him.

The Churches of Galatia appear to have been among the first (perhaps the very first) to receive directions about the collection for the poor at Jerusalem. We learn from 1st Cor. xvi. 1 that they had previously received the order which is there repeated to the Corinthians. *The Epistle to the Galatians.* When, however, the Epistle to the Romans was written, as St. Paul was about to start for Jerusalem with the contributions of the Gentile Churches; the Churches of Macedonia and Achaia were mentioned as contributors, but the Churches of Galatia were passed over in silence. This silence is not, of course, conclusive proof that they were not to be numbered among the contributors, though it is rather ominous; but it derives additional significance from the fact that there is a corresponding silence about the collection in the Epistle to the Galatians, which is shown by very strong internal evidence to have been written shortly before the Epistle to the Romans.*

---

* When the Epistle to the Romans was written the mind of the writer was evidently full of the same ideas which we find in his Epistle to the Galatians. In Galatians iii. 12 we read, "And the law is not of faith: but, The man that doeth them shall live in them"; and in Romans x. 5, "But Moses describeth the righteousness of the law, That the man which doeth those things shall live in them." In Galatians iii. 22, "But the Scripture hath concluded all under sin that the promise by faith of Jesus Christ might be given to them that

The Galatian Epistle closes without any directions about the collection, or any renewal of the invitation to contribute which had been made to them some time before.

The Apostle does indeed mention in Chapter ii. 10 his zeal for the cause of the poor of Jerusalem, but he does not ask the Galatians to help him in the good work. Near the close of the Epistle, in the place where a reference to this collection might have been expected, we have instead a reference to the duty of providing for their own local clergy, which, of course, could not be regarded as any personal compliment to St. Paul; but the direction on this subject is given with a studied brevity and severity of tone which presents a striking contrast to the affectionate appeal at the close of 3rd Corinthians, or even to that which is found in the last Chapter of 1st Corinthians. In Galatians we have only the brief command (Gal. vi. 6) "Let him that is taught in the word communicate unto him that teacheth in all good

---

believe"; and in Romans xi. 32, "But God hath concluded them all in unbelief that He might have mercy upon all." In some passages we not only have the same ideas expressed in almost the same language but also occurring in the same order. We may compare Galatians iii. 14, 15, 29 with Romans iv. 13, 14, 16. Compare also Galatians iv. 6, 7 with Romans viii. 14, 15, 16, 17. Resemblances such as these between these two Epistles cannot have been caused by any resemblance between the occasions of the two letters; for St. Paul had no controversy with the Romans, and his Epistle to them was of the nature of a treatise; while the Epistle to the Galatians is a vehemently controversial letter.

THE VISITS OF TITUS TO CORINTH 127

things"; followed immediately by the stern warning "Be not deceived; God is not mocked: for whatsoever a man soweth, that shall he also reap."

Bishop Wordsworth in his Commentary founds upon this silence an argument for assigning to the Epistle to the Galatians a date earlier than the inception of St. Paul's plans about the collection. The advocates of the later date for this Epistle, while they successfully reply to the Bishop's other arguments, attempt no answer to this, although he dwells upon it at considerable length. It is indeed not easy to imagine what possible reply could be made to it by critics who believed that Titus was commissioned to make arrangements at Corinth for this very collection, when the rebellion there was at its height; and that the affectionate appeals in the later references to this subject were made while the Corinthians were challenging St. Paul's authority and impugning the disinterestedness of his motives, and that they were inserted by him in the same epistle in which he replies to these taunts by declaring that no man "in the regions of Achaia shall stop him of his boasting" that he has never been beholden to them for any pecuniary help.

But the objection of Bishop Wordsworth would never have had any force had not the latter part of the stern second epistle been placed at the close of the Epistle which was written after the réconciliation had taken place, and when Titus had been despatched to Corinth on his final mission to arrange about the collection, as he had during his previous visit arranged the still more important matters which had been entrusted to him. At the close of 2nd Corinthians (A.V. II. ch. x.–xiii.) the collection for Jerusalem is as completely ignored as it is at the close of Galatians; but the union of two manuscripts has obscured this fact by placing the directions which belonged to another letter in their present anomalous position in the middle of the composite epistle. Upon our theory they come in their natural place at the end of the third Epistle (A.V. II. viii. ix.).

In this way we can also explain the otherwise perplexing circumstance that St. Paul when he wrote to Corinth after the reconciliation was evidently doubtful whether the Corinthians were ready, although at some previous period he had boasted that they had been ready a year ago. It would appear from the directions originally given that each man was to be his own treasurer for the money which he laid by each week, and that diocesan treasurers were not to take charge of the contributions before St. Paul's arrival at Corinth. "Upon the first day of the week let each one of you lay by him in store as he may prosper, that collections may not be made after my coming. And when I arrive, whomsoever ye shall approve, them will I send with letters to Jerusalem." Under conditions such as these St. Paul might naturally fear that during the period of anarchy and

ST. PAUL'S DIPLOMACY

confusion which intervened, the collection might have suffered as well as other still more important interests; and that many individual members of the Church, without being conscious of any dishonesty, might have dissipated part of the store which they had previously laid by, looking on it as their own money. Thus, though he had reason to believe that they were ready a year ago, he might not be certain, (and indeed he evidently did not feel certain) that they were ready now.

The Epistle to the Galatians may also help us in another way, by giving us an idea of what the opening of 2nd Corinthians would have been like if it had been preserved for us. *Diplomacy of St. Paul.* A great deal has been said about St. Paul's diplomacy in connection with the Epistles to the Corinthians, and it has been suggested that the extraordinary combination of praise and blame, which has been produced by the fusion of two Epistles in the canonical 2nd Corinthians, is to be explained by his habit of diplomatically softening censure, in saying something complimentary beforehand.

That St. Paul had diplomatic skill is certain; but there are two uses to which such skill may be put. It may be used, and is too often used, to deceive, to convey false impressions of the speaker's meaning, and make his sentiments appear different from what they really are. But it has a worthier use, and one which may be of the greatest importance. It may be employed, not for the purpose of giving a false impression, but for the directly opposite purpose of giving a true impression of the thoughts and feelings of the speaker, guarding skilfully against misunderstanding, and removing it when it already exists. I believe that it was to the latter of these two purposes, and to that alone, that Paul directed his diplomatic skill, whether he had to do with individuals or with Churches. When he was in the power of a governor whose public life was full of oppression and injustice, as was his private life of profligacy, the diplomacy of Paul did not lead him to direct his discourse to those points which would be least likely to give offence, but rather to strike home at the besetting sins of the man with whom he had to deal; so that when Felix sent for him, and heard him concerning the faith in Christ, it was of righteousness, temperance, and judgment to come, that he reasoned till Felix trembled, and cut short the interview.

In dealing with Churches too, when he was on the whole pleased with a Church but had some matters to censure, the first Epistle to the Corinthians shows us what his procedure was. He first tells them in earnest words how he thanks God for what has been wrought in them, and then earnestly entreats them to unity, telling them that he has heard that there are divisions among them.

ST. PAUL'S DIPLOMACY

But the Epistle to the Galatians shows us that when St. Paul was seriously displeased with a Church he did not preface his censure with compliments. Even the opening sentence of that Epistle has an ominous ring, and prepares us for something startling to follow. "Paul an Apostle, not of men, neither by man, but by Jesus Christ and God who raised him from the dead"; then, after bestowing on his readers his blessing, but without a word of preliminary praise, the Apostle in the sixth verse of the first Chapter goes straight at the subject of which his mind was full. The Epistle ends with a blessing, as it began with a blessing, but it also ends, as it began, without a single compliment, or a word of praise.

The Epistle to the Galatians presents the true parallel, and the only parallel which we possess, to the indignation, the vehemence, and the pathos of which 2nd Corinthians x.–xiii. is full, and the parallel which it affords gives us no encouragement to attribute to St. Paul the habit of softening his censure beforehand by compliments so inconsistent and even contradictory as would be the declaration "I rejoice therefore that I have confidence in you in all things" (Chap. vii. 16); if he was about to write in the very same letter "I fear lest, when I come, I shall not find you such as I would, and that I shall be found unto you such as ye would not" (Chap. xii. 20).

It is indeed difficult to see what diplomacy there would be in combining statements so contradictory as these, statements which would afford such material for the accusation of saying "Yea yea and nay nay"; or what could be the object of explaining that to spare them he had not come again unto Corinth, and of going on to show that this was not merely a postponement but an abandonment of his threat,* if the writer intended to repeat later on with earnest emphasis the very threat which he had cancelled "I have warned, and I warn, as when I was present on the second visit, so also when I am absent now, to those who have sinned before and to all the rest, that, if I come again I will not spare." If the writer had changed his mind in the interval, a very moderate amount of diplomatic skill would have suggested omitting the sentence in which the threat had been cancelled, if changed circumstances had rendered it necessary to fall back upon the warning he had intended to revoke.

Nor could a diplomatist like St. Paul (who in the nine Chapters takes such pains to explain any statement or act which might appear to be inconsistent) have left standing the twice repeated assurance that he was not going to commend himself again,

* As he does by the words which follow, "And I determined this for myself that I would not again come to you with sorrow; for if I make you sorry, who is he then that maketh me glad but the same that is made sorry by me?"

ST. PAUL'S DIPLOMACY

if he had found it necessary to commend himself (as he does in Chapters x.–xiii.) at far greater length and in far stronger terms than he had done in 1st Corinthians. He would indeed have a perfect right to cancel the assurance, if the situation had changed from what it was when he wrote it; but the commonest diplomatic prudence would have suggested that it was not advisable to despatch to the Corinthians, without the slightest explanation, the promise and the falsification of the promise by the same messenger, in the same letter. Nor can either the one or the other have been an oversight. They are both too prominent in the letter to admit of this explanation. In the nine Chapters we not only have the assurance that he is not going again to commend himself, but (as we have already seen) we have in the first Chapter a careful explanation of his previous self-commendation, and a declaration that he knows that the Corinthians acknowledge the truth of all that he there has said. His boasting in the four chapters is equally deliberate, for he calls attention to it both by his constant use of the word καυχᾶσθαι, and also by an express statement in xii. 11, where he employs the same verb συνίστασθαι which he employs when assuring them that he will not again commend himself; the reason too which he here assigns is in direct contradiction to the assurance in i. 12 that they do acknowledge him and acknowledge all that he says.

If the declaration in xii. 11 was written before the reconciliation effected by Titus and the explanation in i. 12 after, there is of course no confusion; but if they were both written after that reconciliation and sent in the same letter it would be impossible to suggest any explanation of a contradiction the intentional character of which is nevertheless apparent from the employment of the same terms συνίστασθαι and καύχησις in the contradictory statements.

There is also a grave psychological difficulty in the supposition that indignation and anguish so intense and vehement could have been so long and so completely suppressed through nine Chapters; and that a writer like St. Paul could have maintained during all that time a frame of mind so opposite to those feelings as that which finds utterance in the earnest expressions of approval, of joy, and of thanksgiving with which these Chapters are filled. We have seen how in his Epistle to the Galatians he plunged at once into the subject of which his heart was full; but even in 1st Corinthians, where there is no trace of such vehement emotion, he begins early in the first Chapter the discussion of the points which he wishes to censure, and continues the consideration of them till, in the beginning of the seventh Chapter, he turns to the points which have been suggested by the letter from the Corinthian Church.

INTERNAL AND EXTERNAL EVIDENCE

Among the proofs which I have laid before the reader, I attach most weight to the references in the nine Chapters, (which I have described as 3rd Corinthians) to corresponding passages in the four Chapters, and to the circumstance that in those references, the Apostle speaks in the past tense of acts and plans which in the corresponding passages in the four Chapters are present or future; and that this time order is never reversed. These proofs derive additional weight from the circumstance that the three references in the nine Chapters are all to be found in the very paragraph in which St. Paul expressly refers to the Epistle which he had so lately written to Corinth, and one of them is to be found in the very sentence in which he makes this express mention of his previous letter. We have also seen that all the marks which could have been expected beforehand to be present in documents originally separate, which had been by mistake joined together, are actually present here; we have a sharp contrast of tone, and (a circumstance which is not to be confounded with the preceding one, and which by no means follows from it), we have, at the very point where this change of tone begins, a break not only in the sense, but also in the syntax;

for we have a copulative conjunction which cannot be connected with anything that has preceded it, as the text now stands; and we have an objection alluded to as if it had been spoken of already, yet for which nothing that has gone before prepares us.

A further indication that there has been some displacement of the text is the anomalous position of the Chapters which deal with the subject of the collection, coming before the Chapters, which, if the present composite document were really one epistle, must necessarily be regarded as the most important as well as the most painful part of it, instead of the natural and appropriate position, which they occupy in 1st Corinthians, immediately before the final salutations, and after the writer has disposed of all the important questions of doctrine and discipline which have come before him. Here on the contrary the references to the collection come immediately before the sudden break in sense and syntax, which as the document now stands, ushers in the four Chapters. Additional light on this point seems to be supplied by the sixth and seventh verses of the eighth Chapter which, (taken in their connection with each other), plainly teach us that the collection formed no part of Titus's commission when he was sent to explain and enforce the message of the Epistle which the Apostle had written to Corinth during the revolt against his authority, and that it was only when the Corinthian Church acknowledged his claims and re-

INTERNAL EVIDENCE

turned to their loyalty that Titus was sent back with a commission to encourage the work of the collection among them.

It is not surprising that translators and commentators should have endeavoured by an interpolation in verse 7 to avoid a translation of the two verses which would lead to this conclusion, for it is sharply opposed, not only to the assumption that the epistle brought by Titus was 1st Corinthians with its express directions about the collection, but also to the unity of 2nd Corinthians, as it is found in our Canon. In that document, as we have it now, further directions about this contribution enforced by earnest and affectionate appeals seem to be followed by a long and indignant vindication of the writer's authority, and of his honesty and purpose, which can leave no doubt in the mind of any attentive reader that both the one and the other had been impugned.

The personal character of these epistles, and their references to recent events such as the visits to Corinth of Timothy and Titus, have furnished us with additional and independent tests. Owing to their references to these personal matters they would be full of unexpected pitfalls for a false theory, which had been hastily constructed for a one-sided consideration of some of their features. Yet, instead of this being the case here, it is, on the contrary, the traditional theory whose advocates have found these references full of difficulties; while we have seen how these difficulties one by one disappear when the four Chapters are recognised as part of an epistle earlier in date than the nine.

Nor are these the only difficulties which are thus removed. It has been admitted, (as we have seen), by Klöpper, a leading advocate of the theory of the priority to the date of 1st Corinthians of the intermediate visit of St. Paul to Corinth, that it is surprising that this visit occupies so prominent a place in the four Chapters of 2nd Corinthians while it is never mentioned in 1st Corinthians. For this perplexing difficulty we can now furnish the simple solution, that the visit is not mentioned in 1st Corinthians because it had not taken place when that epistle was written; and that it is prominent in 2nd Corinthians because that was the first epistle which was sent to Corinth by St. Paul after his return from his visit. It also explains the otherwise inexplicable circumstance that the repentance of the majority of the Corinthian Christians is never once mentioned, or so much as hinted at in the four Chapters, though St. Paul would have known so well how to ground on it an effective appeal to the rebels not to dissociate themselves from their fellow Churchmen who had returned to their allegiance, and might also have reminded them that this circumstance would, if they remained impenitent, be an aggravation of their guilt.

We have also seen that an examination of the paragraph in which Paul addresses the minority, shows, not only by the gentleness and delicacy with which he dissuaded them from pressing for further punishment of the offender, but still more by the great importance which he evidently attached to their forgiveness of his offence, that they must have been, in his judgment, persons of a very different, and indeed totally opposite character to that which has been commonly attributed to them.

EXTERNAL EVIDENCE

We have now to enquire what is to be set in the other scale to outweigh this cumulative evidence derived from so many independent sources. There is apparently in many minds an impression that in the opposite scale must be placed the whole weight of external evidence which is derived from all the manuscripts, and all the versions of this epistle, and that this mass of opposing external evidence must outweigh any amount of internal evidence, however seemingly convincing.

There is, in reality, no conflict of evidence here. Evidence in favour of an occurrence cannot be disproved by the evidence of a thousand trustworthy witnesses who visited the spot without seeing anything, if their visit was considerably later than the date of the alleged occurrence. There is not a shred of evidence in any of the manuscripts, versions, or early Christian writers, for the existence of an Epistle to the Corinthians prior to our 1st Corinthians, yet this apparently overwhelming negative evidence does not prevent the majority of Biblical critics from believing that such an epistle once existed, on the strength of a single allusion in 1st Corinthians v. 9. The business of later scribes was simply to copy the manuscript of each epistle as it was delivered to the Church at large by the local Church to which it was originally addressed. If a mistake had been made in the first copy, and the original had been destroyed, they had no means of getting behind the copy to correct the mistake.

To demand from early manuscripts or Christian writers a direct answer to the present question would be to commit the absurdity of supposing that, if a mistake of this kind had been made, the men of that day must have been aware of it; whereas, if they had been aware of the mistake, it would, of course, not have been made, or would have been corrected. Indirectly, however, external testimony might conceivably throw a formidable weight into the opposite scale by showing that 2nd Corinthians was in the hands of the Christian Church at so early a date as to render it improbable that a mistake of this kind could have been made at Corinth, when the recollection of the circumstances

EXTERNAL EVIDENCE

under which the manuscript letters had been received by the Church must have been preserved by some of its members.

Evidence of this kind might also be fairly assumed to show that 1st and 2nd Corinthians must have been published by the Corinthian Church and circulated in the Church at large about the same time, and without apparent hesitation; which would be improbable if some of the manuscripts were perfect, and others in a mutilated condition. If, on the other hand, there is evidence which strongly suggests that 2nd Corinthians must have been given to the world considerably later than 1st Corinthians, this will favour the theory before us in two ways: First it diminishes or altogether removes the improbability that a mistake of this kind could have been made; which is to many minds the strongest objection. Of course the later the date of publication, the less likely would it be that those in authority at Corinth would remember the circumstances under which the manuscripts had originally been received from the Apostle. But indications of this kind would also in another way supply an important link in the evidence. Delay in the publication of a letter, the greater part of which was so complimentary to the Corinthian Church, and so full of affection to them, would be difficult to explain except by the supposition that there was something amiss with the manuscript.

142 SECOND AND THIRD CORINTHIANS

There is only one Christian work external to the Canon of Scripture which is sufficiently early to furnish evidence on this question. Fortunately, however, this one work is addressed to the same Church to which these Epistles were sent. It is also of considerable length; and contains abundant proof that its author was a diligent student of St. Paul's writings as well as of the other Scriptures.

THE EPISTLE OF ST. CLEMENT OF ROME TO THE CORINTHIANS

This epistle was written in the name of the Church of Rome to the Church of Corinth. It is referred to by Hermas, and is recognised by Hegesippus, who speaks of it in connection with his visit to Corinth, and as Dr. Salmon remarks,* probably found it in use there; as for some generations it was read in the Corinthian Church from time to time on Sundays. Bishop Lightfoot has drawn up a table of parallel passages showing the copious use which Polycarp made of this letter,† and the beginning and ending of the letter of the Church of Smyrna about Polycarp's martyrdom are modelled after it. Patrick Young, the first editor (1633),

* *Introduction to the New Testament.*
† *S. Clement of Rome*, by LIGHTFOOT, vol. i. p. 49.

THE EPISTLE OF ST. CLEMENT 143

placed its date about the close of the reign of Domitian, or immediately after (A.D. 95-6). Bishop Lightfoot agreed with this, and remarked that it has so commended itself to critics of various schools and has now become so general that it may be regarded as the received opinion; though some critics have placed it earlier and others later. Harnack in his *Chronologie der Altchristlichen Literatur* (1897) places it between 93 A.D. and 95 A.D.

It is admitted by Lightfoot and other leading critics that this epistle of Clement does not contain a single reference to 2nd Corinthians. This fact shows, at any rate, that the only writer whose date is early enough to enable him to be a witness on this disputed point, does not furnish any external evidence which can be placed in the scale against the internal evidence which has been adduced. We have, however, to enquire whether an examination of the contents of Clement's letter will, or will not, warrant a conclusion which shall go beyond this negative result.

In estimating the force of an argument, which, from the silence of a writer about a particular book of Scripture, infers his ignorance of that book, there are several considerations which have to be attended to. We have to consider the mental characteristics of the later writer, particularly his fondness for quotation, or the reverse; the character of the book of

The Argument from silence.

Scripture in question, and its appropriateness to the subject of which the later writer treats; then we must take account of the circumstances of the persons whom the later writer is addressing and their relation to the book of Scripture, and to its author; and, of course, we must also take into consideration the amount of the writings which we possess from the pen of the later writer. I believe that careful attention to these considerations will show that the argument from silence here is one of altogether exceptional strength.

Clement's epistle shows him to have been a great student of Scripture; as Bishop Lightfoot has remarked, "his knowledge of the Septuagint version is very thorough and intimate. He quotes profusely." With regard to the New Testament, Lightfoot calls attention to Clement's "comprehensiveness" which, as he remarks, "is tested by the range of the Apostolic writings with which the Author is conversant and of which he makes use.... The influence of St. Peter's First Epistle may be traced in more than one passage, while expressions scattered up and down Clement's letter recall the language of several of St. Paul's Epistles belonging to different epochs and representing different types in his literary career. Nor is the comprehensiveness of Clement's letter restricted to a recognition of the two leading Apostles, Peter and Paul. It is so largely interspersed with thoughts and expressions from the

THE EPISTLE OF ST. CLEMENT

Epistle to the Hebrews, that many ancient writers attributed this canonical epistle to Clement. Again the writer shows himself conversant with the type of doctrine and modes of expression characteristic of the Epistle of St. James."* Dr. Lightfoot finally sums up by saying, "We have thus a full recognition of four out of the five types of Apostolic teaching, which confront us in the canonical writings. If the fifth, of which St. John is the exponent, is not clearly affirmed in Clement's letter, the reason is, that the Gospel and Epistles of this Apostle had not yet been written, or if written had not been circulated beyond his own immediate band of personal disciples."

While, however, Clement's Epistle is in many places interspersed with thoughts and expressions from the writings of St. Paul and from the Epistle to the Hebrews, there is only one Book of the New Testament which he expressly names, and that, as we might have anticipated, was a letter of St. Paul to the very Church which Clement was addressing. "Take up,"† he writes, "the epistle of the blessed Paul the Apostle. What wrote he first unto you in the beginning of the Gospel? Of a truth he charged you in the Spirit concerning himself and Cephas and Apollos, because then even then ye had made parties. Yet that making parties brought less sin upon you;

---
* LIGHTFOOT, *St. Clement of Rome*, vol. i. pp. 95-96.
† I quote from Bishop Lightfoot's translation.

for ye were partisans of Apostles that were highly reputed, and of a man approved in their sight. But now, mark ye, who they are that have perverted you and diminished the glory of your renowned love for the brotherhood? It is shameful, dearly beloved, yes, utterly shameful, and unworthy of your conduct in Christ, that it should be reported that the very stedfast and ancient Church of the Corinthians for the sake of one or two persons maketh sedition against its presbyters."

It is not surprising that Clement writing to the Corinthians should desire thus to mark and emphasise his quotation from an epistle which the great Apostle of the Gentiles had addressed to that very Church; nor is it surprising that he should have chosen the particular passage which he has referred to, if he had only that one Epistle to the Corinthians in his own hands. For the party spirit which is rebuked in that passage is perhaps the nearest approach to a parallel which is to be found in 1st Corinthians to the rebellion and sedition which he himself had to rebuke in the same Church now. He shows indeed that he recognises that the parallel is not a close one, and his argument is an argument *a fortiori;* if St. Paul rebuked you for party spirit how much more disgraceful is sedition and rebellion. Now Chapters x.–xiii. of 2nd Corinthians are full of rebukes of the Corinthians for sedition and rebellion —the very sins which Clement had to censure; and

THE EPISTLE OF ST. CLEMENT 147

if it be objected to me that he might from policy have avoided quoting such severe rebukes as are to be found in those chapters; he might at least have found in Chapters i.–ix. warm praise of the same Church for their repentance and submission, of which he might have made effective use in his appeal to them. Yet in the sixty-five Chapters of Clement's epistle there is not a single sentence which indicates that he had ever heard that the Corinthians had before his own time rebelled against those set over them, or that they had ever repented of their rebellion; though he tells the Corinthians that he "has handled every argument."

In addition to the express reference to 1st Corinthians which I have quoted, Clement in other passages in his epistle shows that either his mind was saturated with the language of that epistle, or that he had it open beside him while he wrote and purposely interwove its phraseology with his own. In the forty-ninth Chapter, for instance, he has occasion to mention charity, and at once, his language becomes coloured by the thirteenth Chapter of 1st Corinthians. There are many other instances in his letter. There is at the same time no trace to be found in it of the influence of any passage which is peculiar to 2nd Corinthians. St. Paul in 2nd Corinthians iii. 3 derives a metaphor from Proverbs viii. 3 which he employs in a passage bestowing high praise on the Corinthians. In the passage from which he quotes the Septuagint renders the Hebrew inaccurately, using πλάτος to express the tables of the heart, though πλάξ is the natural equivalent of the Hebrew. Bishop Lightfoot thought that it was not improbable that the "expression arose from a very early corruption of the LXX. text, a confusion of πλάτος and πλακός." St. Paul in 2nd Corinthians iii. 3 avoids the incorrect LXX. rendering, and translates directly from the Hebrew, using the term ἐν πλαξὶ instead of ἐπὶ τὰ πλάτη. Clement, having occasion in his second Chapter to quote this very sentence from Proverbs, does it in a passage which contains no reference to the passage in 2nd Corinthians, and he quotes the incorrect Septuagint rendering, completely ignoring the correct translation of St. Paul.

It is only by reading Clement's letter and by noting how frequently he touches on topics for which apt illustrations and arguments are to be found in both divisions of 2nd Corinthians, that anyone can gain an adequate idea of the extent of the improbability that he could have refrained from making a single allusion to it from beginning to end of the sixty-five Chapters into which his long letter is divided. The force of an argument from silence is (more than other arguments) cumulative. The omission of a reference in any one passage where we might think it suitable, may prove nothing or very little; but it is not so when the passages are

THE EPISTLE OF ST. CLEMENT

multiplied indefinitely, and when the document to which appeal might have been made is an earlier epistle to the same Church to which the later epistle is addressed, and an epistle by the revered founder of that Church, revered alike by the writer and the readers of the later letter. The improbability is still further increased by Clement's fondness for quotation and illustration, and by his evident desire (to use his own words) to "handle every argument."

Among these many passages, however, there is one which is too remarkable to be passed over. In the fifth Chapter Clement wishes to show the Corinthians how "the most righteous pillars of the Church were persecuted, and contended even unto death"; and after speaking of Peter he turns to the consideration of the labours and sufferings of Paul. "By reason of jealousy and strife Paul by his example pointed out the prize of patient endurance. After that he had been seven times in bonds, had been driven into exile, had been stoned, had preached in the East and in the West, had won the noble renown which was the reward of his faith."

In 2nd Corinthians we have a now well-known enumeration of St. Paul's labours and sufferings made by himself. "Of the Jews five times received I forty stripes save one: thrice was I beaten with rods, once was I stoned, thrice I suffered shipwreck, a night and a day I have been in the deep; in journeyings often, in perils of rivers, in perils of robbers, in perils by mine own countrymen, in perils by the heathen, in perils in the City, in perils in the wilderness, in perils in the sea, in perils among false brethren; in weariness and painfulness, in hunger and thirst, in fastings often, in cold and nakedness. Beside those things that are without, that which cometh upon me daily, the care of all the Churches. Who is weak, and I am not weak? Who is offended and I burn not? ... In Damascus the governor of the City under Aretas the king kept the city of the Damascenes with a garrison, desirous to apprehend me: and through a window in a basket was I let down by the wall, and escaped his hands."

Is it conceivable that a man like Clement, when he wished to call the attention of his readers to the greatness of St. Paul's labours and sufferings, would have totally ignored so striking an enumeration of them, if he knew that it had been received by the same Church to which he was writing, from St. Paul himself, and had by them been published and disseminated among the Churches of Christendom? Surely it was an occasion on which he might be expected to say "Take up the epistle of the blessed Paul the Apostle," if he himself had ever previously held that epistle in his hands.

In the closing paragraphs of his letter Clement speaks to the Corinthians of his solicitude for them, and of the joy which he will feel if he receives from them a favourable response. "For ye will give us great joy and gladness if ye render obedience unto the things written by us through the Holy Spirit, and root out the unrighteous anger of your jealousy, according to the entreaty which we have made for peace and concord in this letter. And we have also sent faithful and prudent men that have walked among us from youth to old age unblameably, who shall also be witnesses between you and us, and this we have done that ye might know that we have had, and still have every solicitude that ye should be speedily at peace. . . ." "Now send ye back speedily unto us our messengers Claudius Ephebus and Valerius Bito, together with Fortunatus also, in peace and with joy, to the end that they may the more quickly report the peace and concord which is prayed for and earnestly desired by us, that we also may the more speedily rejoice over your good order."

The position in which Clement at that moment found himself was one to which 3rd Corinthians contains a parallel of the most striking kind. It tells how Paul had, like Clement, looked anxiously for the return of a messenger whom he had despatched to the very same Church; so anxiously that he had no rest in his spirit because he did not find his messenger at Troas, and how he had pressed on from thence into Macedonia that he might sooner receive the report which he expected that Titus would bring from Corinth. Clement's anxiety was, no doubt, less overpowering than Paul's had been. But his letter shows clearly that he was anxious, and to a man like Clement in anxiety about the result of his letter the parallel could not have failed to be an intensely interesting one, and a parallel of the happiest omen. Nor would the interest of the parallel have been merely sentimental. The portion of the Epistle in which St. Paul commends the repentance of the Corinthians, and speaks of the joy which the announcement of it had caused him, would have furnished Clement with arguments of the most telling kind. What effective use might he not have made of such a passage as vii. 9 " Now I rejoice not that ye were made sorry, but that ye sorrowed to repentance; for ye were sorry after a godly manner, that ye might receive damage by us in nothing. For godly sorrow worketh repentance unto salvation not to be repented of!"

This is a parallel of no ordinary kind. There is indeed no other book of the New Testament which bears any comparison with this epistle in the amount of material which it supplies for enforcing Clement's appeal. Yet he, who was so fond of quotation, never once quoted it, and persistently ignored in his letter every circumstance about St. Paul or the Corinthian Church of which it is our sole source of information. There is not a line to show us that he had ever heard of the mission of Titus, or of the rebellion of the

THE PROPOSED SOLUTION 153

Corinthians, or of their repentance and of St. Paul rejoicing over their return to allegiance.

Corinth, both from its nearness to Rome and from the fact of its being a Roman Colony, was in such close communication with the Imperial City that it would be impossible for an epistle of St. Paul which had been published by the Church of Corinth to be unknown to the Church of Rome, or to have totally escaped the notice of so diligent a student of Scripture and so ardent an admirer of St. Paul as the Bishop of Rome was; unless, indeed, it had been published very recently. We may also, I think, dismiss the notion that it could have been published shortly before Clement wrote his letter, for amid the confusion and anarchy which then prevailed in the Church of Corinth it is most improbable that the Corinthians should have had either leisure or inclination to occupy themselves with editing such an epistle.

THE PROBABILITY OR IMPROBABILITY OF THE PROPOSED SOLUTION

I have never seen it expressly stated as extremely improbable that the Corinthian Church can have made the mistake of joining two epistles together in the copies which they issued to the Christian world. I believe, nevertheless, that this a priori assumption is the strongest support of the traditional theory, and that, therefore, no examination of this question can be regarded as complete without an examination of this supposition. The conclusion which the evidence appears to me to suggest is this, that the beginning of the epistle which I have designated as 2nd Corinthians and the end of that which I have spoken of as 3rd Corinthians had from some cause perished, and that the manuscripts being thus imperfect were not given to the world when our 1st Corinthians was published; but that after a considerable interval the suggestion was made by someone that the mutilated manuscripts were really parts of one and the same letter, and that, this suggestion having found favour, they were copied and sent to other Christian Churches in their present form.

If we analyse this conclusion, we may divide it into two parts, which, for the sake of greater clearness, it may be well to consider separately one at a time. The first supposition, then, whose probability or improbability we have to estimate is, that two manuscript letters of St. Paul to Corinth had, before they were copied, lost, the one its beginning and the other its concluding portion.

I do not think that anyone who knows much of manuscripts will seriously assert that this part of the conclusion is in itself improbable. It would appear from 2nd John 12 and 3rd John 13, that some at least of the epistles were written on papyrus, which

THE PROPOSED SOLUTION 155

is a very delicate material and could easily be destroyed by any one of the many accidents to which papers are exposed. Bishop Lightfoot was of opinion that letters of St. Paul to the Philippians have totally perished, and in his note on the subject he reminded his readers that "on the ground of inspiration we cannot assuredly claim for the letters of the Apostle an immunity from the ravages of time, which was denied to the words of the Saviour Himself." But experience teaches us not only generally that papers are perishable, but also that the beginnings and endings of books and manuscripts are the most likely portions to be torn, lost, or otherwise destroyed. For an illustration of this fact we have not to go further than the epistles attributed to Clement, the very author whom we have just been considering. Both these works were, till lately, in a mutilated condition. The First Epistle had lost a leaf near the end, and the so-called Second Epistle all its concluding portion.

Examples of this kind might easily be multiplied, but it would be a needless waste of time to do this in proof of a fact which is so well known, and which, not students of manuscripts only, but most members of the very much larger circle of book owners, have had obtruded on their notice oftener than they would wish.

It cannot be alleged that the information which we possess about the Church of Corinth makes it specially unlikely that such disasters should have happened to manuscripts which were in their care. From everything which we can learn of them it does not appear that order, carefulness, and method were their strong points; so that it would not have been unlikely beforehand that such accidents should occur. But we have also the fact (as is now almost universally admitted) that an epistle referred to in 1st Corinthians v. 9 did actually perish before any copy was made.

To this it may be objected that, however true it may be that there was no antecedent improbability that manuscripts or portions of manuscripts might perish, and though it may be the fact that an epistle which was written before our 1st Corinthians and which was once under the care of the Corinthian Church, has perished, there is, nevertheless, a strong improbability that anything of the kind can have occurred in the case which we are considering, because we have had 2nd Corinthians delivered to us as one letter, whole and complete. We have, therefore, to consider the further question, How far is it improbable that in this case two mutilated manuscripts may have been joined in one document?

The assertion that an alleged event is improbable may be met in two ways. We may adduce evidence (if such is to be had) tending to show that such an event must have actually occurred, however improbable it might beforehand have seemed. This I

THE PROPOSED SOLUTION

have already endeavoured to do, and the proofs which I have adduced have been submitted to my readers in the preceding pages. But we also very fairly meet this objection by suggesting a way in which the event, which is alleged to be improbable, might have occurred. This could not of course be accepted as a substitute for evidence; for to suggest a probable way in which a mistake may have occurred is not the same as proving that it has occurred; but when proof has been already brought forward in support of a conclusion, and has been met by the assertion that the conclusion is in itself too improbable to permit the proof to be seriously considered, a legitimate (and indeed the only direct) way of meeting this particular form of opposition is, to show that the conclusion is not really in itself an improbable one.

We have seen, I think, that it is probable, to a very high degree, that the document which we have known as 2nd Corinthians had not yet been given to the world when Clement wrote his Epistle to Corinth about the year 96 A.D. That epistle informs us that Claudius Ephebus and Valerius Bito were sent at that time as messengers from the Church of Rome to the Church of Corinth, that they might report the result of Clement's letter. Of the result of their mission we have not any explicit information; but the fact that Dionysius, Bishop of Corinth A.D. 170, informs us that Clement's letter was from time to time read on Sundays in the Church of Corinth, makes it more than probable that it was favourably received there. As Clement evidently attached great importance to this mission, and to the settlement of the disorders at Corinth, his messengers would naturally remain there for some days, or perhaps even weeks; and during that time it would be highly improbable that the Corinthian sedition would be the sole subject of conversation, or that other matters of interest would not sometimes be discussed. Among such topics there is none which would more inevitably be suggested than St. Paul's correspondence with Corinth; for Clement's letter would almost force this subject on the attention of the readers of his letter by the words "Take up the epistle of the blessed Paul the Apostle." To intelligent ecclesiastics, such as we may fairly assume Claudius Ephebus and Valerius Bito to have been, it would be most interesting to talk on this subject with members of a Church which had received a letter from the great Apostle of the Gentiles; and to the Corinthians it could not but be pleasant to learn how highly the letter which their Church had received was prized by the Church of the Imperial City. If this subject was often spoken of, it would be most natural that some member of the Corinthian Church who was aware of the existence of fragments of an unpublished letter, or letters, of the Apostle, should mention the fact, and that the news should awaken eager interest in the minds of the visitors, and lead to their being shown the manuscripts. What, then, would they see, according to the hypothesis whose probability we are now testing? Two mutilated manuscripts, of unequal length; the longer manuscript wanting its conclusion and apostolic signature, the shorter wanting its beginning. It would certainly not be improbable that one of the visitors should be struck by the fact that, though there were here apparently two manuscripts, there was only one opening salutation, and one conclusion, and one apostolic signature, and that the idea should occur to him that the shorter manuscript might be the conclusion of the longer one. The idea would thrill him and his companions with joy, for, if true, it would give them a priceless treasure, a complete epistle of St. Paul, a most welcome gift for their bishop, and the Church of Rome, and all the Churches of Christendom. As they further examined the documents with eager interest, they might find the suggestion apparently confirmed by the fact that the longer and shorter manuscripts both seemed to speak of an approaching visit of Paul to Corinth. The references indeed were to visits of very different character; there was a deep-seated discrepancy concealed under a superficial resemblance; but the resemblance would attract attention in a hasty examination made with a strong desire to find confirmation of a discovery which promised so glorious a result. The idea would be almost as welcome to the Corinthians as to the visitors, and the natural result of the conference would be that a skilful scribe or scribes would be set to work to make two copies of the restored epistle, one for the Church of Rome, and one for the Church of Corinth. The epistle when copied would be presented to the Christian Church with the imprimatur of the Church to which it had been originally addressed, and that of the premier Church of Christendom, and would thus, of course, meet with universal acceptance. This would certainly harmonise in a striking way with the fact noticed by Dr. Robertson in his article on 2nd Corinthians in Clark's *Dictionary of the Bible, i.e.* that "the traces of this Epistle in the post-apostolic age are as slight as those of the first Epistle are exceptionally strong," and yet that from the time when it begins to be mentioned it appears to have been received without the slightest doubt, and does not seem to have been absent from any list of writings of St. Paul.*

---

* We possess no Epistle of St. Paul, or of any other Apostle, in an incomplete form; yet it is highly improbable that at the time when the Churches which had received Epistles began to copy them, they had no imperfect manuscripts in their possession. Bishop Lightfoot, in a note on *Lost Epistles to the Philippians*, has remarked that, "if we extend our range of view beyond the Philippians to the many Churches of his founding, if we take into account not these ten years only, but the whole period of his missionary life, we can hardly resist the conclusion that in the epistles of our Canon we have only a part—perhaps not a very large part—of the whole correspondence

THE PROPOSED SOLUTION

I do not, of course, for a moment assert that the mistake must have occurred at the time of the visit of Clement's messengers. All I maintain is that there is no improbability in it, and that therefore the objection which founds itself on the supposed improbability of any such occurrence falls to the ground. The actual date may have been somewhat later, for every time that Clement's letter was publicly read at Corinth it would call the attention of the hearers to St. Paul's correspondence with their city, by the direction to "take up the epistle of the blessed Paul the Apostle." The interval

---

of the Apostle either with Churches or with individuals." Now if we suppose that the letters which we possess were half of the total number which were written and received (and this is apparently a larger proportion than Bishop Lightfoot would have thought probable), it is scarcely possible that all the letters written by St. Paul should have either been preserved intact, or have totally perished by the time when the Churches began to copy his Epistles, probably soon after his martyrdom. According to the law of chances there should be a certain proportion which had neither totally perished nor remained intact, but of which a part was lost; and if this was so, our not having any letters of this kind would appear to be due to the fact that in the first century the authorities of the Churches did not copy any epistles except those which appeared to be perfect. This would account for the delay in the publication of 2nd Corinthians. If the original letter, however, was a single manuscript in a defective condition, it would be plainly impossible for the Church ever to supply the defect, or even to fancy that they could do so. The supposition, which will therefore best explain both the delay in publication and the publication later on, is that to which I believe we are led by a number of circumstances, *i.e.* that there were two or more fragments, which at the time of publication were combined by the copyists.

during which I believe that 2nd Corinthians must have been given to the world has its terminus *a quo* in the date of Clement's letter, and its terminus *ad quem* some time before the date of Polycarp's letter, in which 2nd Corinthians is quoted.

ΠΑΥΛΟΥ ΤΟΥ ΑΠΟΣΤΟΛΟΥ
Η ΠΡΟΣ
ΚΟΡΙΝΘΙΟΥΣ ΕΠΙΣΤΟΛΗ ΔΕΥΤΕΡΑ

* * * * * * * * * * * *
* * * Αὐτὸς δὲ ἐγὼ Παῦλος παρακαλῶ ὑμᾶς διὰ 10 τῆς πραότητος καὶ ἐπιεικείας τοῦ Χριστοῦ, ὃς κατὰ πρόσωπον μὲν ταπεινὸς ἐν ὑμῖν, ἀπὼν δὲ θαρρῶ εἰς ὑμᾶς. δέομαι δέ, τὸ μὴ παρὼν θαρρῆσαι τῇ πεποιθήσει ᾗ 2 λογίζομαι τολμῆσαι ἐπί τινας τοὺς λογιζομένους ἡμᾶς ὡς κατὰ σάρκα περιπατοῦντας. ἐν σαρκὶ γὰρ περιπα- 3 τοῦντες, οὐ κατὰ σάρκα στρατευόμεθα· τὰ γὰρ ὅπλα τῆς 4 στρατείας ἡμῶν οὐ σαρκικά, ἀλλὰ δυνατὰ τῷ Θεῷ πρὸς καθαίρεσιν ὀχυρωμάτων· λογισμοὺς καθαιροῦντες καὶ 5 πᾶν ὕψωμα ἐπαιρόμενον κατὰ τῆς γνώσεως τοῦ Θεοῦ, καὶ αἰχμαλωτίζοντες πᾶν νόημα εἰς τὴν ὑπακοὴν τοῦ Χριστοῦ, καὶ ἐν ἑτοίμῳ ἔχοντες ἐκδικῆσαι πᾶσαν παρα- 6 κοήν, ὅταν πληρωθῇ ὑμῶν ἡ ὑπακοή.

Τὰ κατὰ πρόσωπον βλέπετε; εἴ τις πέποιθεν ἑαυτῷ 7 Χριστοῦ εἶναι, τοῦτο λογιζέσθω πάλιν ἀφ᾽ ἑαυτοῦ, ὅτι καθὼς αὐτὸς Χριστοῦ, οὕτω καὶ ἡμεῖς Χριστοῦ. ἐάν τε 8 γὰρ καὶ περισσότερόν τι καυχήσωμαι περὶ τῆς ἐξουσίας ἡμῶν, ἧς ἔδωκεν ὁ Κύριος ἡμῖν, εἰς οἰκοδομὴν καὶ οὐκ εἰς καθαίρεσιν ὑμῶν, οὐκ αἰσχυνθήσομαι· ἵνα μὴ δόξω 9 ὡς ἂν ἐκφοβεῖν ὑμᾶς διὰ τῶν ἐπιστολῶν. ὅτι αἱ μὲν 10

ἐπιστολαὶ, φησὶ, βαρεῖαι καὶ ἰσχυραί· ἡ δὲ παρουσία τοῦ
11 σώματος ἀσθενὴς, καὶ ὁ λόγος ἐξουθενημένος. τοῦτο
λογιζέσθω ὁ τοιοῦτος, ὅτι οἷοί ἐσμεν τῷ λόγῳ δι' ἐπιστολῶν ἀπόντες, τοιοῦτοι καὶ παρόντες τῷ ἔργῳ.
12 Οὐ γὰρ τολμῶμεν ἐγκρῖναι ἢ συγκρῖναι ἑαυτούς τισι
τῶν ἑαυτοὺς συνιστανόντων, ἀλλὰ αὐτοὶ ἐν ἑαυτοῖς ἑαυτοὺς μετροῦντες, καὶ συγκρίνοντες ἑαυτοὺς ἑαυτοῖς, οὐ
13 συνιοῦσιν. ἡμεῖς δὲ οὐχὶ εἰς τὰ ἄμετρα καυχησόμεθα,
ἀλλὰ κατὰ τὸ μέτρον τοῦ κανόνος οὗ ἐμέρισεν ἡμῖν ὁ
14 Θεὸς μέτρου, ἐφικέσθαι ἄχρι καὶ ὑμῶν· οὐ γὰρ ὡς μὴ
ἐφικνούμενοι εἰς ὑμᾶς ὑπερεκτείνομεν ἑαυτούς· ἄχρι
γὰρ καὶ ὑμῶν ἐφθάσαμεν ἐν τῷ εὐαγγελίῳ τοῦ Χριστοῦ·
15 οὐκ εἰς τὰ ἄμετρα καυχώμενοι ἐν ἀλλοτρίοις κόποις,
ἐλπίδα δὲ ἔχοντες, αὐξανομένης τῆς πίστεως ὑμῶν, ἐν
ὑμῖν μεγαλυνθῆναι, κατὰ τὸν κανόνα ἡμῶν, εἰς περισ-
16 σείαν, εἰς τὰ ὑπερέκεινα ὑμῶν εὐαγγελίσασθαι, οὐκ ἐν
17 ἀλλοτρίῳ κανόνι εἰς τὰ ἕτοιμα καυχήσασθαι. Ὁ δὲ
18 καυχώμενος, ἐν Κυρίῳ καυχάσθω· οὐ γὰρ ὁ ἑαυτὸν
συνιστῶν, ἐκεῖνός ἐστι δόκιμος, ἀλλ' ὃν ὁ Κύριος συν-
ίστησιν.

11 Ὄφελον ἀνείχεσθέ μου μικρὸν τῇ ἀφροσύνῃ· ἀλλὰ
2 καὶ ἀνέχεσθέ μου. ζηλῶ γὰρ ὑμᾶς Θεοῦ ζήλῳ· ἡρμοσάμην
γὰρ ὑμᾶς ἑνὶ ἀνδρὶ παρθένον ἁγνὴν παραστῆσαι τῷ
3 Χριστῷ· φοβοῦμαι δὲ μήπως ὡς ὁ ὄφις Εὔαν ἐξηπάτησεν
ἐν τῇ πανουργίᾳ αὐτοῦ, οὕτω φθαρῇ τὰ νοήματα ὑμῶν
4 ἀπὸ τῆς ἁπλότητος τῆς εἰς τὸν Χριστόν. εἰ μὲν γὰρ ὁ
ἐρχόμενος ἄλλον Ἰησοῦν κηρύσσει ὃν οὐκ ἐκηρύξαμεν, ἢ
πνεῦμα ἕτερον λαμβάνετε ὃ οὐκ ἐλάβετε, ἢ εὐαγγέλιον
5 ἕτερον ὃ οὐκ ἐδέξασθε, καλῶς ἠνείχεσθε. Λογίζομαι γὰρ

μηδὲν ὑστερηκέναι τῶν ὑπερλίαν ἀποστόλων. εἰ δὲ καὶ 6 ἰδιώτης τῷ λόγῳ, ἀλλ' οὐ τῇ γνώσει· ἀλλ' ἐν παντὶ φανερωθέντες ἐν πᾶσιν εἰς ὑμᾶς. ἢ ἁμαρτίαν ἐποίησα, 7 ἐμαυτὸν ταπεινῶν ἵνα ὑμεῖς ὑψωθῆτε, ὅτι δωρεὰν τὸ τοῦ Θεοῦ εὐαγγέλιον εὐηγγελισάμην ὑμῖν; ἄλλας ἐκκλησίας 8 ἐσύλησα, λαβὼν ὀψώνιον πρὸς τὴν ὑμῶν διακονίαν· καὶ παρὼν πρὸς ὑμᾶς καὶ ὑστερηθεὶς, οὐ κατενάρκησα οὐδενός· τὸ γὰρ ὑστέρημά μου προσανεπλήρωσαν οἱ ἀδελφοὶ 9 ἐλθόντες ἀπὸ Μακεδονίας· καὶ ἐν παντὶ ἀβαρῆ ὑμῖν ἐμαυτὸν ἐτήρησα καὶ τηρήσω. ἔστιν ἀλήθεια Χριστοῦ 10 ἐν ἐμοὶ, ὅτι ἡ καύχησις αὕτη οὐ φραγήσεται εἰς ἐμὲ ἐν τοῖς κλίμασι τῆς Ἀχαΐας. διατί; ὅτι οὐκ ἀγαπῶ ὑμᾶς; 11 ὁ Θεὸς οἶδεν. ὃ δὲ ποιῶ, καὶ ποιήσω, ἵνα ἐκκόψω τὴν 12 ἀφορμὴν τῶν θελόντων ἀφορμὴν, ἵνα ἐν ᾧ καυχῶνται, εὑρεθῶσι καθὼς καὶ ἡμεῖς. οἱ γὰρ τοιοῦτοι ψευδαπό- 13 στολοι, ἐργάται δόλιοι, μετασχηματιζόμενοι εἰς ἀποστόλους Χριστοῦ· καὶ οὐ θαυμαστόν· αὐτὸς γὰρ ὁ 14 Σατανᾶς μετασχηματίζεται εἰς ἄγγελον φωτός· οὐ 15 μέγα οὖν εἰ καὶ οἱ διάκονοι αὐτοῦ μετασχηματίζονται ὡς διάκονοι δικαιοσύνης, ὧν τὸ τέλος ἔσται κατὰ τὰ ἔργα αὐτῶν. Πάλιν λέγω, μή τις με δόξῃ ἄφρονα 16 εἶναι· εἰ δὲ μή γε, κἂν ὡς ἄφρονα δέξασθέ με, ἵνα μικρόν τι κἀγὼ καυχήσωμαι. ὃ λαλῶ, οὐ λαλῶ κατὰ 17 Κύριον, ἀλλ' ὡς ἐν ἀφροσύνῃ, ἐν ταύτῃ τῇ ὑποστάσει τῆς καυχήσεως. ἐπεὶ πολλοὶ καυχῶνται κατὰ τὴν 18 σάρκα, κἀγὼ καυχήσομαι. ἡδέως γὰρ ἀνέχεσθε τῶς 19 ἀφρόνων, φρόνιμοι ὄντες· ἀνέχεσθε γὰρ, εἴ τις ὑμᾶς 20 καταδουλοῖ, εἴ τις κατεσθίει, εἴ τις λαμβάνει, εἴ τις ἐπαίρεται, εἴ τις ὑμᾶς εἰς πρόσωπον δέρει. κατὰ ἀτι- 21

ΕΠΙΣΤΟΛΗ

μίαν λέγω, ὡς ὅτι ἡμεῖς ἠσθενήσαμεν· ἐν ᾧ δ' ἄν τιν
22 τολμᾷ, ἐν ἀφροσύνῃ λέγω, τολμῶ κἀγώ. Ἑβραῖοί
εἰσι; κἀγώ· Ἰσραηλῖταί εἰσι; κἀγώ· σπέρμα Ἀβραάμ
23 εἰσι; κἀγώ· διάκονοι Χριστοῦ εἰσι; παραφρονῶν
λαλῶ, ὑπὲρ ἐγώ· ἐν κόποις περισσοτέρως, ἐν πληγαῖς
ὑπερβαλλόντως, ἐν φυλακαῖς περισσοτέρως, ἐν θανάτοις
24 πολλάκις. ὑπὸ Ἰουδαίων πεντάκις τεσσαράκοντα παρὰ
25 μίαν ἔλαβον, τρὶς ἐρραβδίσθην, ἅπαξ ἐλιθάσθην, τρὶς
26 ἐναυάγησα, νυχθήμερον ἐν τῷ βυθῷ πεποίηκα· ὁδοιπο-
ρίαις πολλάκις, κινδύνοις ποταμῶν, κινδύνοις λῃστῶν,
κινδύνοις ἐκ γένους, κινδύνοις ἐξ ἐθνῶν, κινδύνοις ἐν
πόλει, κινδύνοις ἐν ἐρημίᾳ, κινδύνοις ἐν θαλάσσῃ,
27 κινδύνοις ἐν ψευδαδέλφοις· ἐν κόπῳ καὶ μόχθῳ, ἐν
ἀγρυπνίαις πολλάκις, ἐν λιμῷ καὶ δίψει, ἐν νηστείαις
28 πολλάκις, ἐν ψύχει καὶ γυμνότητι· χωρὶς τῶν παρεκτὸς,
ἡ ἐπισύστασίς μου ἡ καθ' ἡμέραν, ἡ μέριμνα πασῶν
29 τῶν ἐκκλησιῶν. τίς ἀσθενεῖ, καὶ οὐκ ἀσθενῶ; τίς σκαν-
30 δαλίζεται, καὶ οὐκ ἐγὼ πυροῦμαι; εἰ καυχᾶσθαι δεῖ, τὰ
31 τῆς ἀσθενείας μου καυχήσομαι. Ὁ Θεὸς καὶ πατὴρ τοῦ
Κυρίου ἡμῶν Ἰησοῦ Χριστοῦ οἶδεν, ὁ ὢν εὐλογητὸς εἰς
32 τοὺς αἰῶνας, ὅτι οὐ ψεύδομαι. ἐν Δαμασκῷ ὁ ἐθνάρχης
Ἀρέτα τοῦ βασιλέως ἐφρούρει τὴν Δαμασκηνῶν πόλιν,
33 πιάσαι με θέλων· καὶ διὰ θυρίδος ἐν σαργάνῃ ἐχαλά-
σθην διὰ τοῦ τείχους, καὶ ἐξέφυγον τὰς χεῖρας αὐτοῦ.
12 Καυχᾶσθαι δὴ οὐ συμφέρει μοι· ἐλεύσομαι γὰρ εἰς
2 ὀπτασίας καὶ ἀποκαλύψεις Κυρίου. οἶδα ἄνθρωπον ἐν
Χριστῷ, πρὸ ἐτῶν δεκατεσσάρων· εἴτε ἐν σώματι, οὐκ
οἶδα· εἴτε ἐκτὸς τοῦ σώματος, οὐκ οἶδα· ὁ Θεὸς οἶδεν·
3 ἁρπαγέντα τὸν τοιοῦτον ἕως τρίτου οὐρανοῦ. καὶ οἶδα

τὸν τοιοῦτον ἄνθρωπον· εἴτε ἐν σώματι, εἴτε ἐκτὸς τοῦ σώματος, οὐκ οἶδα· ὁ Θεὸς οἶδεν· ὅτι ἡρπάγη εἰς τὸν 4 παράδεισον, καὶ ἤκουσεν ἄρρητα ῥήματα, ἃ οὐκ ἐξὸν ἀνθρώπῳ λαλῆσαι. ὑπὲρ τοῦ τοιούτου καυχήσομαι· 5 ὑπὲρ δὲ ἐμαυτοῦ οὐ καυχήσομαι, εἰ μὴ ἐν ταῖς ἀσθενείαις μου. ἐὰν γὰρ θελήσω καυχήσασθαι, οὐκ ἔσομαι 6 ἄφρων· ἀλήθειαν γὰρ ἐρῶ· φείδομαι δὲ, μή τις εἰς ἐμὲ λογίσηται ὑπὲρ ὃ βλέπει με, ἢ ἀκούει τι ἐξ ἐμοῦ.

Καὶ τῇ ὑπερβολῇ τῶν ἀποκαλύψεων ἵνα μὴ ὑπεραί-7 ρωμαι, ἐδόθη μοι σκόλοψ τῇ σαρκὶ, ἄγγελος Σατᾶν ἵνα με κολαφίζῃ, ἵνα μὴ ὑπεραίρωμαι. ὑπὲρ τούτου τρὶς τὸν 8 Κύριον παρεκάλεσα, ἵνα ἀποστῇ ἀπ' ἐμοῦ· καὶ εἴρηκέ 9 μοι, Ἀρκεῖ σοι ἡ χάρις μου· ἡ γὰρ δύναμίς μου ἐν ἀσθενείᾳ τελειοῦται. ἥδιστα οὖν μᾶλλον καυχήσομαι ἐν ταῖς ἀσθενείαις μου, ἵνα ἐπισκηνώσῃ ἐπ' ἐμὲ ἡ δύναμις τοῦ Χριστοῦ. διὸ εὐδοκῶ ἐν ἀσθενείαις, ἐν 10 ὕβρεσιν, ἐν ἀνάγκαις, ἐν διωγμοῖς, ἐν στενοχωρίαις, ὑπὲρ Χριστοῦ· ὅταν γὰρ ἀσθενῶ, τότε δυνατός εἰμι. Γέγονα ἄφρων καυχώμενος· ὑμεῖς με ἠναγκάσατε. ἐγὼ 11 γὰρ ὤφειλον ὑφ' ὑμῶν συνίστασθαι· οὐδὲν γὰρ ὑστέρησα τῶν ὑπερλίαν ἀποστόλων, εἰ καὶ οὐδέν εἰμι.

Τὰ μὲν σημεῖα τοῦ ἀποστόλου κατειργάσθη ἐν ὑμῖν 12 ἐν πάσῃ ὑπομονῇ, ἐν σημείοις καὶ τέρασι καὶ δυνάμεσι. τί γάρ ἐστιν ὃ ἡττήθητε ὑπὲρ τὰς λοιπὰς ἐκκλησίας, εἰ 13 μὴ ὅτι αὐτὸς ἐγὼ οὐ κατενάρκησα ὑμῶν; χαρίσασθέ μοι τὴν ἀδικίαν ταύτην. ἰδοὺ τρίτον ἑτοίμως ἔχω ἐλθεῖν 14 πρὸς ὑμᾶς, καὶ οὐ καταναρκήσω ὑμῶν· οὐ γὰρ ζητῶ τὰ ὑμῶν, ἀλλ' ὑμᾶς. οὐ γὰρ ὀφείλει τὰ τέκνα τοῖς γονεῦσι θησαυρίζειν, ἀλλ' οἱ γονεῖς τοῖς τέκνοις· ἐγὼ δὲ ἥδιστα 15

δαπανήσω καὶ ἐκδαπανηθήσομαι ὑπὲρ τῶν ψυχῶν ὑμῶν·
εἰ καὶ περισσοτέρως ὑμᾶς ἀγαπῶν, ἧττον ἀγαπῶμαι.
16 Ἔστω δὲ, ἐγὼ οὐ κατεβάρησα ὑμᾶς. ἀλλ᾽ ὑπάρχων
17 πανοῦργος, δόλῳ ὑμᾶς ἔλαβον. μή τινα ὧν ἀπέσταλκα
18 πρὸς ὑμᾶς, δι᾽ αὐτοῦ ἐπλεονέκτησα ὑμᾶς; παρεκάλεσα
Τίτον, καὶ συναπέστειλα τὸν ἀδελφόν· μήτι ἐπλεονέ-
κτησεν ὑμᾶς Τίτος; οὐ τῷ αὐτῷ πνεύματι περιεπατή-
σαμεν; οὐ τοῖς αὐτοῖς ἴχνεσι;
19 Πάλιν δοκεῖτε ὅτι ὑμῖν ἀπολογούμεθα; κατενώπιον
τοῦ Θεοῦ, ἐν Χριστῷ λαλοῦμεν· τὰ δὲ πάντα ἀγαπητοὶ,
20 ὑπὲρ τῆς ὑμῶν οἰκοδομῆς. φοβοῦμαι γὰρ, μή πως ἐλθὼν
οὐχ οἵους θέλω εὕρω ὑμᾶς, κἀγὼ εὑρεθῶ ὑμῖν οἷον οὐ
θέλετε· μήπως ἔρεις, ζῆλοι, θυμοὶ, ἐριθεῖαι, καταλαλιαὶ,
21 ψιθυρισμοὶ, φυσιώσεις, ἀκαταστασίαι· μὴ πάλιν ἐλθόντα
με ταπεινώσῃ ὁ Θεός μου πρὸς ὑμᾶς, καὶ πενθήσω πολλοὺς τῶν προημαρτηκότων, καὶ μὴ μετανοησάντων ἐπὶ
τῇ ἀκαθαρσίᾳ καὶ πορνείᾳ καὶ ἀσελγείᾳ ᾗ ἔπραξαν.
13 Τρίτον τοῦτο ἔρχομαι πρὸς ὑμᾶς· ἐπὶ στόματος
2 δύο μαρτύρων καὶ τριῶν σταθήσεται πᾶν ῥῆμα. προείρηκα καὶ προλέγω, ὡς παρὼν τὸ δεύτερον, καὶ ἀπὼν
νῦν γράφω, τοῖς προημαρτηκόσι καὶ τοῖς λοιποῖς πᾶσιν,
3 ὅτι ἐὰν ἔλθω εἰς τὸ πάλιν, οὐ φείσομαι· ἐπεὶ δοκιμὴν
ζητεῖτε τοῦ ἐν ἐμοὶ λαλοῦντος Χριστοῦ, ὃς εἰς ὑμᾶς οὐκ
4 ἀσθενεῖ, ἀλλὰ δυνατεῖ ἐν ὑμῖν. καὶ γὰρ εἰ ἐσταυρώθη
ἐξ ἀσθενείας, ἀλλὰ ζῇ ἐκ δυνάμεως Θεοῦ· καὶ γὰρ
ἡμεῖς ἀσθενοῦμεν ἐν αὐτῷ, ἀλλὰ ζησόμεθα σὺν αὐτῷ
5 ἐκ δυνάμεως Θεοῦ εἰς ὑμᾶς. ἑαυτοὺς πειράζετε εἰ ἐστὲ
ἐν τῇ πίστει, ἑαυτοὺς δοκιμάζετε· ἢ οὐκ ἐπιγινώσκετε
ἑαυτοὺς, ὅτι Ἰησοῦς Χριστὸς ἐν ὑμῖν ἐστιν; εἰ μήτι

ἀδόκιμοί ἐστε. ἐλπίζω δὲ ὅτι γνώσεσθε ὅτι ἡμεῖς οὐκ 6
ἐσμὲν ἀδόκιμοι. εὔχομαι δὲ πρὸς τὸν Θεὸν, μὴ ποιῆσαι 7
ὑμᾶς κακὸν μηδέν, οὐχ ἵνα ἡμεῖς δόκιμοι φανῶμεν,
ἀλλ' ἵνα ὑμεῖς τὸ καλὸν ποιῆτε, ἡμεῖς δὲ ὡς ἀδόκιμοι
ὦμεν. οὐ γὰρ δυνάμεθά τι κατὰ τῆς ἀληθείας, ἀλλ' 8
ὑπὲρ τῆς ἀληθείας. χαίρομεν γὰρ ὅταν ἡμεῖς ἀσθενῶ- 9
μεν, ὑμεῖς δὲ δυνατοὶ ἦτε· τοῦτο δὲ καὶ εὐχόμεθα, τὴν
ὑμῶν κατάρτισιν. διὰ τοῦτο ταῦτα ἀπὼν γράφω, ἵνα 10
παρὼν μὴ ἀποτόμως χρήσωμαι, κατὰ τὴν ἐξουσίαν ἣν
ἔδωκέ μοι ὁ Κύριος εἰς οἰκοδομὴν, καὶ οὐκ εἰς καθαίρεσιν.

Λοιπὸν ἀδελφοὶ, χαίρετε, καταρτίζεσθε, παρακαλεῖσθε, 11
τὸ αὐτὸ φρονεῖτε, εἰρηνεύετε· καὶ ὁ Θεὸς τῆς ἀγάπης
καὶ εἰρήνης ἔσται μεθ' ὑμῶν. Ἀσπάσασθε ἀλλήλους 12
ἐν ἁγίῳ φιλήματι· ἀσπάζονται ὑμᾶς οἱ ἅγιοι πάντες.
Ἡ χάρις τοῦ Κυρίου Ἰησοῦ Χριστοῦ, καὶ ἡ ἀγάπη τοῦ 13
Θεοῦ, καὶ ἡ κοινωνία τοῦ Ἁγίου Πνεύματος μετὰ πάντων ὑμῶν. ἀμήν.

ΠΑΥΛΟΥ ΤΟΥ ΑΠΟΣΤΟΛΟΥ
Η ΠΡΟΣ
ΚΟΡΙΝΘΙΟΥΣ ΕΠΙΣΤΟΛΗ ΤΡΙΤΗ

1 Παῦλος ἀπόστολος Ἰησου Χριστοῦ, διὰ θελήματος Θεοῦ, καὶ Τιμόθεος ὁ ἀδελφὸς, τῇ ἐκκλησίᾳ τοῦ Θεοῦ τῇ οὔσῃ ἐν Κορίνθῳ, σὺν τοῖς ἁγίοις πᾶσι τοῖς οὖσιν ἐν 2 ὅλῃ τῇ Ἀχαΐᾳ· χάρις ὑμῖν καὶ εἰρήνη ἀπὸ Θεοῦ πατρὸς ἡμῶν καὶ Κυρίου Ἰησοῦ Χριστοῦ.

3 Εὐλογητὸς ὁ Θεὸς καὶ πατὴρ τοῦ Κυρίου ἡμῶν Ἰησοῦ Χριστοῦ, ὁ πατὴρ τῶν οἰκτιρμῶν καὶ Θεὸς πάσης παρα- 4 κλήσεως, ὁ παρακαλῶν ἡμᾶς ἐπὶ πάσῃ τῇ θλίψει ἡμῶν, εἰς τὸ δύνασθαι ἡμᾶς παρακαλεῖν τοὺς ἐν πάσῃ θλίψει, διὰ τῆς παρακλήσεως ἧς παρακαλούμεθα αὐτοὶ ὑπὸ τοῦ 5 Θεοῦ· ὅτι καθὼς περισσεύει τὰ παθήματα τοῦ Χριστοῦ εἰς ἡμᾶς, οὕτω διὰ Χριστοῦ περισσεύει καὶ ἡ παράκλησις 6 ἡμῶν. εἴτε δὲ θλιβόμεθα, ὑπὲρ τῆς ὑμῶν παρακλήσεως καὶ σωτηρίας, τῆς ἐνεργουμένης ἐν ὑπομονῇ τῶν αὐτῶν παθημάτων ὧν καὶ ἡμεῖς πάσχομεν· εἴτε παρακαλούμεθα, ὑπὲρ τῆς ὑμῶν παρακλήσεως καὶ σωτηρίας· καὶ ἡ 7 ἐλπὶς ἡμῶν βεβαία ὑπὲρ ὑμῶν· εἰδότες ὅτι ὥσπερ κοινωνοί ἐστε τῶν παθημάτων, οὕτω καὶ τῆς παρακλήσεως. 8 Οὐ γὰρ θέλομεν ὑμᾶς ἀγνοεῖν ἀδελφοὶ, ὑπὲρ τῆς θλίψεως ἡμῶν τῆς γενομένης ἡμῖν ἐν τῇ Ἀσίᾳ, ὅτι καθ᾽

ΠΡΟΣ ΚΟΡΙΝΘΙΟΥΣ Γ

ὑπερβολὴν ἐβαρήθημεν ὑπὲρ δύναμιν, ὥστε ἐξαπορηθῆναι ἡμᾶς καὶ τοῦ ζῆν· ἀλλὰ αὐτοὶ ἐν ἑαυτοῖς τὸ ἀπό- 9 κριμα τοῦ θανάτου ἐσχήκαμεν, ἵνα μὴ πεποιθότες ὦμεν ἐφ' ἑαυτοῖς, ἀλλ' ἐπὶ τῷ Θεῷ τῷ ἐγείροντι τοὺς νεκρούς· 10 ὃς ἐκ τηλικούτου θανάτου ἐρρύσατο ἡμᾶς καὶ ῥύεται, εἰς ὃν ἠλπίκαμεν ὅτι καὶ ἔτι ῥύσεται, συνυπουργούντων καὶ 11 ὑμῶν ὑπὲρ ἡμῶν τῇ δεήσει, ἵνα ἐκ πολλῶν προσώπων τὸ εἰς ἡμᾶς χάρισμα διὰ πολλῶν εὐχαριστηθῇ ὑπὲρ ἡμῶν.

Ἡ γὰρ καύχησις ἡμῶν αὕτη ἐστὶ τὸ μαρτύριον τῆς 12 συνειδήσεως ἡμῶν, ὅτι ἐν ἁπλότητι καὶ εἰλικρινείᾳ Θεοῦ, οὐκ ἐν σοφίᾳ σαρκικῇ, ἀλλ' ἐν χάριτι Θεοῦ ἀνεστράφημεν ἐν τῷ κόσμῳ, περισσοτέρως δὲ πρὸς ὑμᾶς. οὐ γὰρ ἄλλα γράφομεν ὑμῖν, ἀλλ' ἢ ἃ ἀναγινώσκετε, ἢ 13 καὶ ἐπιγινώσκετε, ἐλπίζω δὲ ὅτι καὶ ἕως τέλους ἐπιγνώσεσθε, καθὼς καὶ ἐπέγνωτε ἡμᾶς ἀπὸ μέρους, ὅτι 14 καύχημα ὑμῶν ἐσμεν, καθάπερ καὶ ὑμεῖς ἡμῶν, ἐν τῇ ἡμέρᾳ τοῦ Κυρίου Ἰησοῦ. Καὶ ταύτῃ τῇ πεποιθήσει 15 ἐβουλόμην πρὸς ὑμᾶς ἐλθεῖν πρότερον, ἵνα δευτέραν χάριν ἔχητε· καὶ δι' ὑμῶν διελθεῖν εἰς Μακεδονίαν, καὶ πάλιν 16 ἀπὸ Μακεδονίας ἐλθεῖν πρὸς ὑμᾶς, καὶ ὑφ' ὑμῶν προπεμφθῆναι εἰς τὴν Ἰουδαίαν. τοῦτο οὖν βουλευόμενος, 17 μήτι ἄρα τῇ ἐλαφρίᾳ ἐχρησάμην; ἢ ἃ βουλεύομαι, κατὰ σάρκα βουλεύομαι, ἵνα ᾖ παρ' ἐμοὶ τὸ ναὶ ναὶ, καὶ τὸ οὒ οὔ; πιστὸς δὲ ὁ Θεὸς, ὅτι ὁ λόγος ἡμῶν ὁ πρὸς ὑμᾶς 18 οὐκ ἐγένετο ναὶ καὶ οὔ· ὁ γὰρ τοῦ Θεοῦ υἱὸς Ἰησοῦς 19 Χριστὸς ὁ ἐν ὑμῖν δι' ἡμῶν κηρυχθεὶς, δι' ἐμοῦ καὶ Σιλουανοῦ καὶ Τιμοθέου, οὐκ ἐγένετο ναὶ καὶ οὒ, ἀλλὰ ναὶ ἐν αὐτῷ γέγονεν· ὅσαι γὰρ ἐπαγγελίαι Θεοῦ, ἐν 20

αὐτῷ τὸ ναὶ, καὶ ἐν αὐτῷ τὸ ἀμὴν, τῷ Θεῷ πρὸς δόξαν
21 δι' ἡμῶν. ὁ δὲ βεβαιῶν ἡμᾶς σὺν ὑμῖν εἰς Χριστὸν, καὶ
22 χρίσας ἡμᾶς, Θεός· ὁ καὶ σφραγισάμενος ἡμᾶς, καὶ δοὺς
τὸν ἀρραβῶνα τοῦ πνεύματος ἐν ταῖς καρδίαις ἡμῶν.
23 Ἐγὼ δὲ μάρτυρα τὸν Θεὸν ἐπικαλοῦμαι ἐπὶ τὴν ἐμὴν
ψυχὴν, ὅτι φειδόμενος ὑμῶν οὐκέτι ἦλθον εἰς Κόρινθον·
24 οὐχ ὅτι κυριεύομεν ὑμῶν τῆς πίστεως, ἀλλὰ συνεργοί
2 ἐσμεν τῆς χαρᾶς ὑμῶν, τῇ γὰρ πίστει ἐστήκατε· ἔκρινα
δὲ ἐμαυτῷ τοῦτο, τὸ μὴ πάλιν ἐν λύπῃ πρὸς ὑμᾶς
2 ἐλθεῖν. εἰ γὰρ ἐγὼ λυπῶ ὑμᾶς, καὶ τίς ἐστιν ὁ
3 εὐφραίνων με, εἰ μὴ ὁ λυπούμενος ἐξ ἐμοῦ; καὶ ἔγραψα
ὑμῖν τοῦτο αὐτὸ, ἵνα μὴ ἐλθὼν λύπην ἔχω ἀφ' ὧν ἔδει με
χαίρειν· πεποιθὼς ἐπὶ πάντας ὑμᾶς, ὅτι ἡ ἐμὴ χαρὰ
4 πάντων ὑμῶν ἐστιν. ἐκ γὰρ πολλῆς θλίψεως καὶ συνοχῆς
καρδίας ἔγραψα ὑμῖν διὰ πολλῶν δακρύων, οὐχ ἵνα λυπη-
θῆτε, ἀλλὰ τὴν ἀγάπην ἵνα γνῶτε ἣν ἔχω περισσοτέρως
εἰς ὑμᾶς.

5 Εἰ δέ τις λελύπηκεν, οὐκ ἐμὲ λελύπηκεν, ἀλλ' ἀπὸ
6 μέρους, ἵνα μὴ ἐπιβαρῶ πάντας ὑμᾶς. ἱκανὸν τῷ τοιούτῳ
7 ἡ ἐπιτιμία αὕτη ἡ ὑπὸ τῶν πλειόνων· ὥστε τοὐναντίον
μᾶλλον ὑμᾶς χαρίσασθαι καὶ παρακαλέσαι, μήπως τῇ
8 περισσοτέρᾳ λύπῃ καταποθῇ ὁ τοιοῦτος. διὸ παρακαλῶ
9 ὑμᾶς κυρῶσαι εἰς αὐτὸν ἀγάπην· εἰς τοῦτο γὰρ καὶ
ἔγραψα, ἵνα γνῶ τὴν δοκιμὴν ὑμῶν, εἰ εἰς πάντα ὑπή-
10 κοοί ἐστε. ᾧ δέ τι χαρίζεσθε, καὶ ἐγώ· καὶ γὰρ ἐγὼ
εἴ τι κεχάρισμαι, ᾧ κεχάρισμαι, δι' ὑμᾶς, ἐν προσώπῳ
11 Χριστοῦ, ἵνα μὴ πλεονεκτηθῶμεν ὑπὸ τοῦ Σατανᾶ· οὐ
γὰρ αὐτοῦ τὰ νοήματα ἀγνοοῦμεν.
12 Ἐλθὼν δὲ εἰς τὴν Τρωάδα εἰς τὸ εὐαγγέλιον τοῦ

ΠΡΟΣ ΚΟΡΙΝΘΙΟΥΣ Γ

Χριστοῦ, καὶ θύρας μοι ἀνεῳγμένης ἐν Κυρίῳ, οὐκ 13 ἔσχηκα ἄνεσιν τῷ πνεύματί μου, τῷ μὴ εὑρεῖν με Τίτον τὸν ἀδελφόν μου· ἀλλὰ ἀποταξάμενος αὐτοῖς, ἐξῆλθον εἰς Μακεδονίαν. Τῷ δὲ Θεῷ χάρις τῷ πάντοτε θριαμ- 14 βεύοντι ἡμᾶς ἐν τῷ Χριστῷ, καὶ τὴν ὀσμὴν τῆς γνώσεως αὐτοῦ φανεροῦντι δι' ἡμῶν ἐν παντὶ τόπῳ. ὅτι Χριστοῦ 15 εὐωδία ἐσμὲν τῷ Θεῷ ἐν τοῖς σωζομένοις καὶ ἐν τοῖς ἀπολλυμένοις· οἷς μὲν, ὀσμὴ θανάτου εἰς θάνατον· οἷς 16 δὲ, ὀσμὴ ζωῆς εἰς ζωήν. καὶ πρὸς ταῦτα τίς ἱκανός; οὐ 17 γάρ ἐσμεν ὡς οἱ πολλοί, καπηλεύοντες τὸν λόγον τοῦ Θεοῦ, ἀλλ' ὡς ἐξ εἰλικρινείας, ἀλλ' ὡς ἐκ Θεοῦ, κατενώπιον τοῦ Θεοῦ, ἐν Χριστῷ λαλοῦμεν. Ἀρχόμεθα 3 πάλιν ἑαυτοὺς συνιστάνειν; εἰ μὴ χρῄζομεν, ὥς τινες, συστατικῶν ἐπιστολῶν πρὸς ὑμᾶς, ἢ ἐξ ὑμῶν συστατικῶν; ἡ ἐπιστολὴ ἡμῶν ὑμεῖς ἐστε, ἐγγεγραμμένη ἐν 2 ταῖς καρδίαις ἡμῶν, γινωσκομένη καὶ ἀναγινωσκομένη ὑπὸ πάντων ἀνθρώπων· φανερούμενοι ὅτι ἐστὲ ἐπιστολὴ 3 Χριστοῦ διακονηθεῖσα ὑφ' ἡμῶν, ἐγγεγραμμένη οὐ μέλανι, ἀλλὰ πνεύματι Θεοῦ ζῶντος, οὐκ ἐν πλαξὶ λιθίναις, ἀλλὰ ἐν πλαξὶ καρδίας σαρκίναις. Πεποίθησιν 4 δὲ τοιαύτην ἔχομεν διὰ τοῦ Χριστοῦ πρὸς τὸν Θεόν· οὐχ ὅτι ἱκανοί ἐσμεν ἀφ' ἑαυτῶν λογίσασθαί τι, ὡς ἐξ 5 ἑαυτῶν, ἀλλ' ἡ ἱκανότης ἡμῶν ἐκ τοῦ Θεοῦ· ὃς καὶ ἱκά- 6 νωσεν ἡμᾶς διακόνους καινῆς διαθήκης, οὐ γράμματος, ἀλλὰ πνεύματος· τὸ γὰρ γράμμα ἀποκτείνει, τὸ δὲ πνεῦμα ζωοποιεῖ. Εἰ δὲ ἡ διακονία τοῦ θανάτου ἐν 7 γράμμασιν ἐντετυπωμένη ἐν λίθοις, ἐγενήθη ἐν δόξῃ, ὥστε μὴ δύνασθαι ἀτενίσαι τοὺς υἱοὺς Ἰσραὴλ εἰς τὸ πρόσωπον Μωσέως, διὰ τὴν δόξαν τοῦ προσώπου αὐτοῦ

8 τὴν καταργουμένην· πῶς οὐχὶ μᾶλλον ἡ διακονία τοῦ
9 πνεύματος ἔσται ἐν δόξῃ; εἰ γὰρ ἡ διακονία τῆς κατακρίσεως δόξα, πολλῷ μᾶλλον περισσεύει ἡ διακονία τῆς
10 δικαιοσύνης ἐν δόξῃ. καὶ γὰρ οὐδὲ δεδόξασται τὸ δεδοξασμένον ἐν τούτῳ τῷ μέρει, ἕνεκεν τῆς ὑπερβαλ-
11 λούσης δόξης. εἰ γὰρ τὸ καταργούμενον, διὰ δόξης·
12 πολλῷ μᾶλλον τὸ μένον, ἐν δόξῃ. Ἔχοντες οὖν τοιαύ-
13 την ἐλπίδα, πολλῇ παρρησίᾳ χρώμεθα· καὶ οὐ καθάπερ
Μωσῆς ἐτίθει κάλυμμα ἐπὶ τὸ πρόσωπον ἑαυτοῦ, πρὸς
τὸ μὴ ἀτενίσαι τοὺς υἱοὺς Ἰσραὴλ εἰς τὸ τέλος τοῦ
14 καταργουμένου· ἀλλ' ἐπωρώθη τὰ νοήματα αὐτῶν. ἄχρι
γὰρ τῆς σήμερον τὸ αὐτὸ κάλυμμα ἐπὶ τῇ ἀναγνώσει
τῆς παλαιᾶς διαθήκης μένει μὴ ἀνακαλυπτόμενον, ὅτι
15 ἐν Χριστῷ καταργεῖται· ἀλλ' ἕως σήμερον, ἡνίκα ἀναγινώσκεται Μωσῆς, κάλυμμα ἐπὶ τὴν καρδίαν αὐτῶν
16 κεῖται· ἡνίκα δ' ἂν ἐπιστρέψῃ πρὸς Κύριον, περιαιρεῖται
17 τὸ κάλυμμα. Ὁ δὲ Κύριος τὸ πνεῦμά ἐστιν· οὗ δὲ τὸ
18 πνεῦμα Κυρίου, ἐκεῖ ἐλευθερία. ἡμεῖς δὲ πάντες ἀνακεκαλυμμένῳ προσώπῳ τὴν δόξαν Κυρίου κατοπτριζόμενοι, τὴν αὐτὴν εἰκόνα μεταμορφούμεθα ἀπὸ δόξης εἰς
4 δόξαν, καθάπερ ἀπὸ Κυρίου πνεύματος. Διὰ τοῦτο
ἔχοντες τὴν διακονίαν ταύτην, καθὼς ἠλεήθημεν, οὐκ
2 ἐκκακοῦμεν, ἀλλ' ἀπειπάμεθα τὰ κρυπτὰ τῆς αἰσχύνης,
μὴ περιπατοῦντες ἐν πανουργίᾳ, μηδὲ δολοῦντες τὸν
λόγον τοῦ Θεοῦ, ἀλλὰ τῇ φανερώσει τῆς ἀληθείας
συνιστῶντες ἑαυτοὺς πρὸς πᾶσαν συνείδησιν ἀνθρώπων,
3 ἐνώπιον τοῦ Θεοῦ. Εἰ δὲ καὶ ἔστι κεκαλυμμένον τὸ
εὐαγγέλιον ἡμῶν, ἐν τοῖς ἀπολλυμένοις ἐστὶ κεκαλυμ-
4 μένον· ἐν οἷς ὁ θεὸς τοῦ αἰῶνος τούτου ἐτύφλωσε τὰ

ΠΡΟΣ ΚΟΡΙΝΘΙΟΥΣ Γ

νοήματα τῶν ἀπίστων, εἰς τὸ μὴ αὐγάσαι αὐτοῖς τὸν φωτισμὸν τοῦ εὐαγγελίου τῆς δόξης τοῦ Χριστοῦ, ὅς ἐστιν εἰκὼν τοῦ Θεοῦ. οὐ γὰρ ἑαυτοὺς κηρύσσομεν, 5 ἀλλὰ Χριστὸν Ἰησοῦν Κύριον· ἑαυτοὺς δὲ δούλους ὑμῶν διὰ Ἰησοῦν· ὅτι ὁ Θεὸς ὁ εἰπὼν ἐκ σκότους φῶς 6 λάμψαι, ὃς ἔλαμψεν ἐν ταῖς καρδίαις ἡμῶν, πρὸς φωτισμὸν τῆς γνώσεως τῆς δόξης τοῦ Θεοῦ ἐν προσώπῳ Ἰησοῦ Χριστοῦ.

Ἔχομεν δὲ τὸν θησαυρὸν τοῦτον ἐν ὀστρακίνοις σκεύ- 7 εσιν, ἵνα ἡ ὑπερβολὴ τῆς δυνάμεως ᾖ τοῦ Θεοῦ, καὶ μὴ ἐξ ἡμῶν· ἐν παντὶ θλιβόμενοι, ἀλλ' οὐ στενοχωρού- 8 μενοι· ἀπορούμενοι, ἀλλ' οὐκ ἐξαπορούμενοι· διωκόμε- 9 νοι, ἀλλ' οὐκ ἐγκαταλειπόμενοι· καταβαλλόμενοι, ἀλλ' οὐκ ἀπολλύμενοι· πάντοτε τὴν νέκρωσιν τοῦ Κυρίου 10 Ἰησοῦ ἐν τῷ σώματι περιφέροντες, ἵνα καὶ ἡ ζωὴ τοῦ Ἰησοῦ ἐν τῷ σώματι ἡμῶν φανερωθῇ. ἀεὶ γὰρ ἡμεῖς οἱ 11 ζῶντες εἰς θάνατον παραδιδόμεθα διὰ Ἰησοῦν, ἵνα καὶ ἡ ζωὴ τοῦ Ἰησοῦ φανερωθῇ ἐν τῇ θνητῇ σαρκὶ ἡμῶν. Ὥστε ὁ μὲν θάνατος ἐν ἡμῖν ἐνεργεῖται, ἡ δὲ ζωὴ ἐν 12 ὑμῖν. ἔχοντες δὲ τὸ αὐτὸ πνεῦμα τῆς πίστεως, κατὰ 13 τὸ γεγραμμένον, Ἐπίστευσα, διὸ ἐλάλησα, καὶ ἡμεῖς πιστεύομεν, διὸ καὶ λαλοῦμεν· εἰδότες ὅτι ὁ ἐγείρας 14 τὸν Κύριον Ἰησοῦν, καὶ ἡμᾶς διὰ Ἰησοῦ ἐγερεῖ, καὶ παραστήσει σὺν ὑμῖν. τὰ γὰρ πάντα δι' ὑμᾶς, ἵνα ἡ 15 χάρις πλεονάσασα, διὰ τῶν πλειόνων τὴν εὐχαριστίαν περισσεύσῃ εἰς τὴν δόξαν τοῦ Θεοῦ. Διὸ οὐκ ἐκκα- 16 κοῦμεν· ἀλλ' εἰ καὶ ὁ ἔξω ἡμῶν ἄνθρωπος διαφθείρεται, ἀλλ' ὁ ἔσωθεν ἀνακαινοῦται ἡμέρᾳ καὶ ἡμέρᾳ. τὸ γὰρ 17 παραυτίκα ἐλαφρὸν τῆς θλίψεως ἡμῶν καθ' ὑπερβολὴν

ΕΠΙΣΤΟΛΗ

εἰς ὑπερβολὴν αἰώνιον βάρος δόξης κατεργάζεται ἡμῖν,
18 μὴ σκοπούντων ἡμῶν τὰ βλεπόμενα, ἀλλὰ τὰ μὴ βλεπόμενα· τὰ γὰρ βλεπόμενα πρόσκαιρα· τὰ δὲ μὴ βλε-
5 πόμενα αἰώνια. οἴδαμεν γὰρ, ὅτι ἐὰν ἡ ἐπίγειος ἡμῶν οἰκία τοῦ σκήνους καταλυθῇ, οἰκοδομὴν ἐκ Θεοῦ ἔχομεν,
2 οἰκίαν ἀχειροποίητον, αἰώνιον, ἐν τοῖς οὐρανοῖς. καὶ γὰρ ἐν τούτῳ στενάζομεν, τὸ οἰκητήριον ἡμῶν τὸ ἐξ οὐρανοῦ
3 ἐπενδύσασθαι ἐπιποθοῦντες. εἴ γε καὶ ἐνδυσάμενοι, οὐ
4 γυμνοὶ εὑρεθησόμεθα. καὶ γὰρ οἱ ὄντες ἐν τῷ σκήνει στενάζομεν βαρούμενοι· ἐπειδὴ οὐ θέλομεν ἐκδύσασθαι, ἀλλ' ἐπενδύσασθαι, ἵνα καταποθῇ τὸ θνητὸν ὑπὸ τῆς
5 ζωῆς. ὁ δὲ κατεργασάμενος ἡμᾶς εἰς αὐτὸ τοῦτο Θεὸς, ὁ
6 καὶ δοὺς ἡμῖν τὸν ἀρραβῶνα τοῦ πνεύματος. θαρροῦντες οὖν πάντοτε, καὶ εἰδότες ὅτι ἐνδημοῦντες ἐν τῷ σώματι,
7 ἐκδημοῦμεν ἀπὸ τοῦ Κυρίου· διὰ πίστεως γὰρ περιπα-
8 τοῦμεν, οὐ διὰ εἴδους· θαρροῦμεν δὲ καὶ εὐδοκοῦμεν μᾶλλον ἐκδημῆσαι ἐκ τοῦ σώματος, καὶ ἐνδημῆσαι πρὸς τὸν Κύριον.
9 Διὸ καὶ φιλοτιμούμεθα, εἴτε ἐνδημοῦντες, εἴτε ἐκδη-
10 μοῦντες, εὐάρεστοι αὐτῷ εἶναι. τοὺς γὰρ πάντας ἡμᾶς φανερωθῆναι δεῖ ἔμπροσθεν τοῦ βήματος τοῦ Χριστοῦ, ἵνα κομίσηται ἕκαστος τὰ διὰ τοῦ σώματος, πρὸς ἃ
11 ἔπραξεν, εἴτε ἀγαθὸν, εἴτε κακόν. εἰδότες οὖν τὸν φόβον τοῦ Κυρίου, ἀνθρώπους πείθομεν· Θεῷ δὲ πεφανερώμεθα· ἐλπίζω δὲ καὶ ἐν ταῖς συνειδήσεσιν ὑμῶν
12 πεφανερῶσθαι. οὐ γὰρ πάλιν ἑαυτοὺς συνιστάνομεν ὑμῖν, ἀλλὰ ἀφορμὴν διδόντες ὑμῖν καυχήματος ὑπὲρ ἡμῶν, ἵνα ἔχητε πρὸς τοὺς ἐν προσώπῳ καυχωμένους,
13 καὶ οὐ καρδίᾳ. εἴτε γὰρ ἐξέστημεν, Θεῷ· εἴτε σωφρο-

νοῦμεν, ὑμῖν. Ἡ γὰρ ἀγάπη τοῦ Χριστοῦ συνέχει ἡμᾶς, 14 κρίναντας τοῦτο, ὅτι εἰ εἷς ὑπὲρ πάντων ἀπέθανεν, ἄρα 15 οἱ πάντες ἀπέθανον· καὶ ὑπὲρ πάντων ἀπέθανεν, ἵνα οἱ ζῶντες μηκέτι ἑαυτοῖς ζῶσιν, ἀλλὰ τῷ ὑπὲρ αὐτῶν ἀποθανόντι καὶ ἐγερθέντι. ὥστε ἡμεῖς ἀπὸ τοῦ νῦν οὐδένα 16 οἴδαμεν κατὰ σάρκα· εἰ δὲ καὶ ἐγνώκαμεν κατὰ σάρκα Χριστὸν, ἀλλὰ νῦν οὐκ ἔτι γινώσκομεν. ὥστε εἴ τις ἐν 17 Χριστῷ, καινὴ κτίσις· τὰ ἀρχαῖα παρῆλθεν, ἰδοὺ γέγονε καινὰ τὰ πάντα. Τὰ δὲ πάντα ἐκ τοῦ Θεοῦ, τοῦ καταλ- 18 λάξαντος ἡμᾶς ἑαυτῷ διὰ Ἰησοῦ Χριστοῦ, καὶ δόντος ἡμῖν τὴν διακονίαν τῆς καταλλαγῆς· ὡς ὅτι Θεὸς ἦν ἐν 19 Χριστῷ κόσμον καταλλάσσων ἑαυτῷ, μὴ λογιζόμενος αὐτοῖς τὰ παραπτώματα αὐτῶν, καὶ θέμενος ἐν ἡμῖν τὸν λόγον τῆς καταλλαγῆς. Ὑπὲρ Χριστοῦ οὖν πρεσβεύο- 20 μεν, ὡς τοῦ Θεοῦ παρακαλοῦντος δι' ἡμῶν· δεόμεθα ὑπὲρ Χριστοῦ, καταλλάγητε τῷ Θεῷ· τὸν γὰρ μὴ γνόντα 21 ἁμαρτίαν, ὑπὲρ ἡμῶν ἁμαρτίαν ἐποίησεν, ἵνα ἡμεῖς γινώμεθα δικαιοσύνη Θεοῦ ἐν αὐτῷ. συνεργοῦντες δὲ 6 καὶ παρακαλοῦμεν, μὴ εἰς κενὸν τὴν χάριν τοῦ Θεοῦ δέξασθαι ὑμᾶς· λέγει γὰρ, Καιρῷ δεκτῷ ἐπήκουσά σου, 2 καὶ ἐν ἡμέρᾳ σωτηρίας ἐβοήθησά σοι· ἰδοὺ νῦν καιρὸς εὐπρόσδεκτος, ἰδοὺ νῦν ἡμέρα σωτηρίας· μηδεμίαν ἐν 3 μηδενὶ διδόντες προσκοπὴν, ἵνα μὴ μωμηθῇ ἡ διακονία· ἀλλ' ἐν παντὶ συνιστῶντες ἑαυτοὺς ὡς Θεοῦ διάκονοι, 4 ἐν ὑπομονῇ πολλῇ, ἐν θλίψεσιν, ἐν ἀνάγκαις, ἐν στενοχωρίαις, ἐν πληγαῖς, ἐν φυλακαῖς, ἐν ἀκαταστασίαις, ἐν 5 κόποις, ἐν ἀγρυπνίαις, ἐν νηστείαις, ἐν ἁγνότητι, ἐν 6 γνώσει, ἐν μακροθυμίᾳ, ἐν χρηστότητι, ἐν Πνεύματι Ἁγίῳ, ἐν ἀγάπῃ ἀνυποκρίτῳ, ἐν λόγῳ ἀληθείας, ἐν δυ- 7

ΕΠΙΣΤΟΛΗ

νάμει Θεοῦ, διὰ τῶν ὅπλων τῆς δικαιοσύνης τῶν δεξιῶν
8 καὶ ἀριστερῶν, διὰ δόξης καὶ ἀτιμίας, διὰ δυσφημίας καὶ
9 εὐφημίας· ὡς πλάνοι, καὶ ἀληθεῖς· ὡς ἀγνοούμενοι, καὶ
ἐπιγινωσκόμενοι· ὡς ἀποθνήσκοντες, καὶ ἰδοὺ ζῶμεν· ὡς
10 παιδευόμενοι, καὶ μὴ θανατούμενοι· ὡς λυπούμενοι, ἀεὶ
δὲ χαίροντες· ὡς πτωχοί, πολλοὺς δὲ πλουτίζοντες· ὡς
μηδὲν ἔχοντες, καὶ πάντα κατέχοντες.

11 Τὸ στόμα ἡμῶν ἀνέῳγε πρὸς ὑμᾶς Κορίνθιοι, ἡ καρδία
12 ἡμῶν πεπλάτυνται· οὐ στενοχωρεῖσθε ἐν ἡμῖν, στενο-
13 χωρεῖσθε δὲ ἐν τοῖς σπλάγχνοις ὑμῶν· τὴν δὲ αὐτὴν
ἀντιμισθίαν, ὡς τέκνοις λέγω, πλατύνθητε καὶ ὑμεῖς.
14 Μὴ γίνεσθε ἑτεροζυγοῦντες ἀπίστοις· τίς γὰρ μετοχὴ
15 δικαιοσύνῃ καὶ ἀνομίᾳ; τίς δὲ κοινωνία φωτὶ πρὸς σκό-
τος; τίς δὲ συμφώνησις Χριστῷ πρὸς Βελίαρ; ἢ τίς
16 μερὶς πιστῷ μετὰ ἀπίστου; τίς δὲ συγκατάθεσις ναῷ
Θεοῦ μετὰ εἰδώλων; ὑμεῖς γὰρ ναὸς Θεοῦ ἐστε ζῶντος,
καθὼς εἶπεν ὁ Θεός, Ὅτι ἐνοικήσω ἐν αὐτοῖς, καὶ ἐμ-
περιπατήσω, καὶ ἔσομαι αὐτῶν Θεός· καὶ αὐτοὶ ἔσονταί
17 μοι λαός. διὸ ἐξέλθετε ἐκ μέσου αὐτῶν καὶ ἀφορίσθητε,
18 λέγει Κύριος, καὶ ἀκαθάρτου μὴ ἅπτεσθε· κἀγὼ εἰσ-
δέξομαι ὑμᾶς, καὶ ἔσομαι ὑμῖν εἰς πατέρα, καὶ ὑμεῖς
ἔσεσθέ μοι εἰς υἱοὺς καὶ θυγατέρας, λέγει Κύριος παν-
7 τοκράτωρ. ταύτας οὖν ἔχοντες τὰς ἐπαγγελίας ἀγα-
πητοί, καθαρίσωμεν ἑαυτοὺς ἀπὸ παντὸς μολυσμοῦ σαρ-
κὸς καὶ πνεύματος, ἐπιτελοῦντες ἁγιωσύνην ἐν φόβῳ
Θεοῦ.
2 Χωρήσατε ἡμᾶς· οὐδένα ἠδικήσαμεν, οὐδένα ἐφθεί-
3 ραμεν, οὐδένα ἐπλεονεκτήσαμεν. οὐ πρὸς κατάκρισιν
λέγω· προείρηκα γὰρ ὅτι ἐν ταῖς καρδίαις ἡμῶν ἐστε εἰς

ΠΡΟΣ ΚΟΡΙΝΘΙΟΥΣ Γ 179

τὸ συναποθανεῖν καὶ συζῆν. πολλή μοι παρρησία πρὸς 4 ὑμᾶς, πολλή μοι καύχησις ὑπὲρ ὑμῶν· πεπλήρωμαι τῇ παρακλήσει, ὑπερπερισσεύομαι τῇ χαρᾷ ἐπὶ πάσῃ τῇ θλίψει ἡμῶν. Καὶ γὰρ ἐλθόντων ἡμῶν εἰς Μακεδονίαν, 5 οὐδεμίαν ἔσχηκεν ἄνεσιν ἡ σὰρξ ἡμῶν, ἀλλ' ἐν παντὶ θλιβόμενοι· ἔξωθεν μάχαι, ἔσωθεν φόβοι. ἀλλ' ὁ 6 παρακαλῶν τοὺς ταπεινοὺς παρεκάλεσεν ἡμᾶς ὁ Θεὸς ἐν τῇ παρουσίᾳ Τίτου· οὐ μόνον δὲ ἐν τῇ παρουσίᾳ 7 αὐτοῦ, ἀλλὰ καὶ ἐν τῇ παρακλήσει ᾗ παρεκλήθη ἐφ' ὑμῖν, ἀναγγέλλων ἡμῖν τὴν ὑμῶν ἐπιπόθησιν, τὸν ὑμῶν ὀδυρμόν, τὸν ὑμῶν ζῆλον ὑπὲρ ἐμοῦ, ὥστε με μᾶλλον χαρῆναι. Ὅτι εἰ καὶ ἐλύπησα ὑμᾶς ἐν τῇ ἐπιστολῇ, οὐ 8 μεταμέλομαι, εἰ καὶ μετεμελόμην· βλέπω γὰρ ὅτι ἡ ἐπιστολὴ ἐκείνη εἰ καὶ πρὸς ὥραν ἐλύπησεν ὑμᾶς. Νῦν 9 χαίρω, οὐχ ὅτι ἐλυπήθητε, ἀλλ' ὅτι ἐλυπήθητε εἰς μετάνοιαν· ἐλυπήθητε γὰρ κατὰ Θεόν, ἵνα ἐν μηδενὶ ζημιωθῆτε ἐξ ἡμῶν. ἡ γὰρ κατὰ Θεὸν λύπη μετάνοιαν εἰς 10 σωτηρίαν ἀμεταμέλητον κατεργάζεται· ἡ δὲ τοῦ κόσμου λύπη θάνατον κατεργάζεται. ἰδοὺ γὰρ αὐτὸ τοῦτο τὸ 11 κατὰ Θεὸν λυπηθῆναι ὑμᾶς, πόσην κατειργάσατο ὑμῖν σπουδήν; ἀλλὰ ἀπολογίαν, ἀλλὰ ἀγανάκτησιν· ἀλλὰ φόβον, ἀλλὰ ἐπιπόθησιν· ἀλλὰ ζῆλον, ἀλλ' ἐκδίκησιν. ἐν παντὶ συνεστήσατε ἑαυτοὺς ἁγνοὺς εἶναι ἐν τῷ πράγματι. ἄρα εἰ καὶ ἔγραψα ὑμῖν, οὐχ εἵνεκεν τοῦ ἀδική-12 σαντος, οὐδὲ εἵνεκεν τοῦ ἀδικηθέντος· ἀλλ' εἵνεκεν τοῦ φανερωθῆναι τὴν σπουδὴν ὑμῶν τὴν ὑπὲρ ἡμῶν πρὸς ὑμᾶς ἐνώπιον τοῦ Θεοῦ. Διὰ τοῦτο παρακεκλήμεθα ἐπὶ 13 τῇ παρακλήσει ὑμῶν· περισσοτέρως δὲ μᾶλλον ἐχάρημεν ἐπὶ τῇ χαρᾷ Τίτου, ὅτι ἀναπέπαυται τὸ πνεῦμα αὐτοῦ

ΕΠΙΣΤΟΛΗ

14 ἀπὸ πάντων ὑμῶν· ὅτι εἴ τι αὐτῷ ὑπὲρ ὑμῶν κεκαύχημαι,
οὐ κατῃσχύνθην· ἀλλ᾽ ὡς πάντα ἐν ἀληθείᾳ ἐλαλήσαμεν
ὑμῖν, οὕτω καὶ ἡ καύχησις ἡμῶν ἡ ἐπὶ Τίτου, ἀλήθεια
15 ἐγενήθη· καὶ τὰ σπλάγχνα αὐτοῦ περισσοτέρως εἰς ὑμᾶς
ἐστιν, ἀναμιμνησκομένου τὴν πάντων ὑμῶν ὑπακοὴν, ὡς
16 μετὰ φόβου καὶ τρόμου ἐδέξασθε αὐτόν. χαίρω ὅτι ἐν
παντὶ θαρρῶ ἐν ὑμῖν.

8 Γνωρίζομεν δὲ ὑμῖν ἀδελφοὶ, τὴν χάριν τοῦ Θεοῦ τὴν
2 δεδομένην ἐν ταῖς ἐκκλησίαις τῆς Μακεδονίας· ὅτι ἐν
πολλῇ δοκιμῇ θλίψεως ἡ περισσεία τῆς χαρᾶς αὐτῶν,
καὶ ἡ κατὰ βάθους πτωχεία αὐτῶν ἐπερίσσευσεν εἰς
3 τὸν πλοῦτον τῆς ἁπλότητος αὐτῶν· ὅτι κατὰ δύναμιν,
4 μαρτυρῶ, καὶ ὑπὲρ δύναμιν αὐθαίρετοι, μετὰ πολλῆς
παρακλήσεως δεόμενοι ἡμῶν, τὴν χάριν καὶ τὴν κοινω-
νίαν τῆς διακονίας τῆς εἰς τοὺς ἁγίους δέξασθαι ἡμᾶς,
5 καὶ οὐ καθὼς ἠλπίσαμεν, ἀλλ᾽ ἑαυτοὺς ἔδωκαν πρῶτον
6 τῷ Κυρίῳ, καὶ ἡμῖν διὰ θελήματος Θεοῦ· εἰς τὸ παρακαλέσαι ἡμᾶς Τίτον, ἵνα καθὼς προενήρξατο, οὕτω καὶ
7 ἐπιτελέσῃ, εἰς ὑμᾶς καὶ τὴν χάριν ταύτην. Ἀλλ᾽ ὥσπερ
ἐν παντὶ περισσεύετε, πίστει καὶ λόγῳ καὶ γνώσει καὶ
πάσῃ σπουδῇ, καὶ τῇ ἐξ ὑμῶν ἐν ἡμῖν ἀγάπῃ, ἵνα καὶ ἐν
8 ταύτῃ τῇ χάριτι περισσεύητε· οὐ κατ᾽ ἐπιταγὴν λέγω,
ἀλλὰ διὰ τῆς ἑτέρων σπουδῆς καὶ τὸ τῆς ὑμετέρας ἀγά-
9 πης γνήσιον δοκιμάζων· γινώσκετε γὰρ τὴν χάριν τοῦ
Κυρίου ἡμῶν Ἰησοῦ Χριστοῦ, ὅτι δι᾽ ὑμᾶς ἐπτώχευσε
πλούσιος ὤν, ἵνα ὑμεῖς τῇ ἐκείνου πτωχείᾳ πλουτήσητε·
10 καὶ γνώμην ἐν τούτῳ δίδωμι. τοῦτο γὰρ ὑμῖν συμφέρει,
οἵτινες οὐ μόνον τὸ ποιῆσαι, ἀλλὰ καὶ τὸ θέλειν προε-
11 νήρξασθε ἀπὸ πέρυσι· νυνὶ δὲ καὶ τὸ ποιῆσαι ἐπιτελέ-

ΠΡΟΣ ΚΟΡΙΝΘΙΟΥΣ Γ

σατε, ὅπως καθάπερ ἡ προθυμία τοῦ θέλειν, οὕτω καὶ τὸ
ἐπιτελέσαι ἐκ τοῦ ἔχειν. Εἰ γὰρ ἡ προθυμία πρόκειται, 12
καθὸ ἐὰν ἔχῃ τις, εὐπρόσδεκτος, οὐ καθὸ οὐκ ἔχει. οὐ 13
γὰρ ἵνα ἄλλοις ἄνεσις, ὑμῖν δὲ θλῖψις· ἀλλ' ἐξ ἰσότητος,
ἐν τῷ νῦν καιρῷ τὸ ὑμῶν περίσσευμα εἰς τὸ ἐκείνων
ὑστέρημα· ἵνα καὶ τὸ ἐκείνων περίσσευμα γένηται εἰς 14
τὸ ὑμῶν ὑστέρημα, ὅπως γένηται ἰσότης· καθὼς γέ- 15
γραπται, Ὁ τὸ πολὺ, οὐκ ἐπλεόνασε· καὶ ὁ τὸ ὀλίγον,
οὐκ ἠλαττόνησε.

Χάρις δὲ τῷ Θεῷ τῷ διδόντι τὴν αὐτὴν σπουδὴν 16
ὑπὲρ ὑμῶν ἐν τῇ καρδίᾳ Τίτου· ὅτι τὴν μὲν παράκλησιν 17
ἐδέξατο, σπουδαιότερος δὲ ὑπάρχων, αὐθαίρετος ἐξῆλθε
πρὸς ὑμᾶς. Συνεπέμψαμεν δὲ μετ' αὐτοῦ τὸν ἀδελφὸν, 18
οὗ ὁ ἔπαινος ἐν τῷ εὐαγγελίῳ διὰ πασῶν τῶν ἐκκλησιῶν·
οὐ μόνον δὲ, ἀλλὰ καὶ χειροτονηθεὶς ὑπὸ τῶν ἐκκλησιῶν 19
συνέκδημος ἡμῶν, σὺν τῇ χάριτι ταύτῃ τῇ διακονουμένῃ
ὑφ' ἡμῶν, πρὸς τὴν αὐτοῦ τοῦ Κυρίου δόξαν καὶ προθυμίαν ὑμῶν· στελλόμενοι τοῦτο, μή τις ἡμᾶς μωμήσηται 20
ἐν τῇ ἁδρότητι ταύτῃ τῇ διακονουμένῃ ὑφ' ἡμῶν· προ- 21
νοούμενοι καλὰ οὐ μόνον ἐνώπιον Κυρίου, ἀλλὰ καὶ
ἐνώπιον ἀνθρώπων. Συνεπέμψαμεν δὲ αὐτοῖς τὸν ἀδελ- 22
φὸν ἡμῶν, ὃν ἐδοκιμάσαμεν ἐν πολλοῖς πολλάκις σπου-
δαῖον ὄντα, νυνὶ δὲ πολὺ σπουδαιότερον· πεποιθήσει
πολλῇ τῇ εἰς ὑμᾶς. εἴτε ὑπὲρ Τίτου, κοινωνὸς ἐμὸς καὶ 23
εἰς ὑμᾶς συνεργός· εἴτε ἀδελφοὶ ἡμῶν, ἀπόστολοι ἐκκλησιῶν, δόξα Χριστοῦ. Τὴν οὖν ἔνδειξιν τῆς ἀγάπης ὑμῶν, 24
καὶ ἡμῶν καυχήσεως ὑπὲρ ὑμῶν, εἰς αὐτοὺς ἐνδείξασθε,
καὶ εἰς πρόσωπον τῶν ἐκκλησιῶν. Περὶ μὲν γὰρ τῆς 9
διακονίας τῆς εἰς τοὺς ἁγίους περισσόν μοι ἐστὶ τὸ γρά-

2 φειν ὑμῖν. οἶδα γὰρ τὴν προθυμίαν ὑμῶν, ἣν ὑπὲρ ὑμῶν καυχῶμαι Μακεδόσιν, ὅτι Ἀχαΐα παρεσκεύασται ἀπὸ πέρυσι· καὶ ὁ ἐξ ὑμῶν ζῆλος ἠρέθισε τοὺς πλείονας· 3 ἔπεμψα δὲ τοὺς ἀδελφοὺς, ἵνα μὴ τὸ καύχημα ἡμῶν τὸ ὑπὲρ ὑμῶν κενωθῇ ἐν τῷ μέρει τούτῳ· ἵνα καθὼς ἔλεγον, 4 παρεσκευασμένοι ἦτε, μή πως ἐὰν ἔλθωσι σὺν ἐμοὶ Μακεδόνες, καὶ εὕρωσιν ὑμᾶς ἀπαρασκευάστους, καταισχυνθῶμεν ἡμεῖς, ἵνα μὴ λέγωμεν ὑμεῖς, ἐν τῇ ὑποστάσει 5 ταύτῃ τῆς καυχήσεως. ἀναγκαῖον οὖν ἡγησάμην παρακαλέσαι τοὺς ἀδελφοὺς, ἵνα προέλθωσιν εἰς ὑμᾶς, καὶ προκαταρτίσωσι τὴν προκατηγγελμένην εὐλογίαν ὑμῶν ταύτην ἑτοίμην εἶναι, οὕτως ὡς εὐλογίαν, καὶ μὴ ὥσπερ 6 πλεονεξίαν. Τοῦτο δὲ, ὁ σπείρων φειδομένως, φειδομένως καὶ θερίσει· καὶ ὁ σπείρων ἐπ' εὐλογίαις, ἐπ' 7 εὐλογίαις καὶ θερίσει· ἕκαστος καθὼς προαιρεῖται τῇ καρδίᾳ· μὴ ἐκ λύπης ἢ ἐξ ἀνάγκης· ἱλαρὸν γὰρ δότην 8 ἀγαπᾷ ὁ Θεός. δυνατὸς δὲ ὁ Θεὸς πᾶσαν χάριν περισσεῦσαι εἰς ὑμᾶς, ἵνα ἐν παντὶ πάντοτε πᾶσαν αὐτάρκειαν 9 ἔχοντες, περισσεύητε εἰς πᾶν ἔργον ἀγαθόν· καθὼς γέγραπται, Ἐσκόρπισεν, ἔδωκε τοῖς πένησιν, ἡ δικαιο- 10 σύνη αὐτοῦ μένει εἰς τὸν αἰῶνα· ὁ δὲ ἐπιχορηγῶν σπέρμα τῷ σπείροντι, καὶ ἄρτον εἰς βρῶσιν χορηγήσαι, καὶ πληθύναι τὸν σπόρον ὑμῶν, καὶ αὐξήσαι τὰ γεννή- 11 ματα τῆς δικαιοσύνης ὑμῶν. ἐν παντὶ πλουτιζόμενοι εἰς πᾶσαν ἁπλότητα, ἥτις κατεργάζεται δι' ἡμῶν εὐχαριστίαν 12 τῷ Θεῷ· ὅτι ἡ διακονία τῆς λειτουργίας ταύτης οὐ μόνον ἐστὶ προσαναπληροῦσα τὰ ὑστερήματα τῶν ἁγίων, ἀλλὰ καὶ περισσεύουσα διὰ πολλῶν εὐχαριστιῶν τῷ 13 Θεῷ, διὰ τῆς δοκιμῆς τῆς διακονίας ταύτης δοξάζοντες

τὸν Θεὸν ἐπὶ τῇ ὑποταγῇ τῆς ὁμολογίας ὑμῶν εἰς τὸ εὐαγγέλιον τοῦ Χριστοῦ, καὶ ἁπλότητι τῆς κοινωνίας εἰς αὐτοὺς καὶ εἰς πάντας, καὶ αὐτῶν δεήσει ὑπὲρ ὑμῶν, 14 ἐπιποθούντων ὑμᾶς διὰ τὴν ὑπερβάλλουσαν χάριν τοῦ Θεοῦ ἐφ' ὑμῖν.

χάρις τῷ Θεῷ ἐπὶ τῇ ἀνεκδιηγήτῳ αὐτοῦ δωρεᾷ. 15

THE SECOND EPISTLE OF PAUL THE APOSTLE TO THE CORINTHIANS

* * * * * * * * * * * *

10 * * * * * * But I myself, Paul, who when we are face to face am humble among you, but when I am absent am bold toward you, beseech you 2 by the meekness and gentleness of Christ. But I beseech you, that I may not be bold when I am present with that confidence, wherewith I think to be bold against some, which think of us as if we walked according to 3 the flesh. For though we walk in the flesh, we do not 4 war after the flesh: (for the weapons of our warfare are not carnal, but mighty through God to the pulling down 5 of strong holds;) casting down imaginations, and every high thing that exalteth itself against the knowledge of God, and bringing into captivity every thought to the 6 obedience of Christ; and having in a readiness to revenge 7 all disobedience, when your obedience is fulfilled. Do ye look on things after the outward appearance? If any man trust to himself that he is Christ's, let him of himself think this again, that, as he is Christ's, even so are we 8 Christ's. For though I should boast somewhat more of our authority, which the Lord hath given us for edification, and not for your destruction, I should not be ashamed: 9 that I may not seem as if I would terrify you by letters. 10 For his letters, say they, are weighty and powerful; but his bodily presence is weak, and his speech contemptible.

II. CORINTHIANS

Let such an one think this, that, such as we are in word 11
by letters when we are absent, such will we be also in
deed when we are present. For we dare not make our-12
selves of the number, or compare ourselves with some that
commend themselves: but they measuring themselves by
themselves, and comparing themselves among themselves,
are not wise. But we will not boast of things without our 13
measure, but according to the measure of the rule which
God hath distributed to us, a measure to reach even unto
you. For we stretch not ourselves beyond our measure, as 14
though we reached not unto you: for we are come as far
as to you also in preaching the gospel of Christ: not 15
boasting of things without our measure, that is, of other
men's labours; but having hope, when your faith is increased, that we shall be enlarged by you according to our
rule abundantly. To preach gospel unto the lands on the 16
other side of you, and not to boast in another man's line
of things made ready to our hand. But he that glorieth, 17
let him glory in the Lord. For not he that commendeth 18
himself is approved, but whom the Lord commendeth.

Would to God ye could bear with me a little in my folly: **11**
and indeed bear with me. For I am jealous over you with 2
godly jealousy: for I have espoused you to one husband,
that I may present you as a chaste virgin to Christ. But 3
I fear, lest by any means, as the serpent beguiled Eve
through his subtilty, so your minds should be corrupted
from the simplicity that is in Christ. For if he that cometh 4
preacheth another Jesus, whom we have not preached, or
if ye receive another spirit, which ye have not received,
or another gospel, which ye have not accepted, ye might
well bear with him. For I suppose I was not a whit 5
behind the very chiefest apostles. But though I be rude 6
in speech, yet not in knowledge; but we have been

II. CORINTHIANS

7 thoroughly made manifest among you in all things. Have I committed an offence in abasing myself that ye might be exalted, because I have preached to you the gospel of 8 God freely? I robbed other churches, taking wages of 9 them, to do you service. And when I was present with you, and wanted, I was chargeable to no man; for that which was lacking to me the brethren which came from Macedonia supplied: and in all things I have kept myself from being burdensome unto you, and so will I keep 10 myself. As the truth of Christ is in me, no man shall 11 stop me of this boasting in the regions of Achaia. Where-12 fore? because I love you not? God knoweth. But what I do, that I will do, that I may cut off occasion from them which desire occasion; that wherein they glory, they may 13 be found even as we. For such are false apostles, deceitful workers, transforming themselves into the apostles of Christ. 14 And no marvel; for Satan himself is transformed into an 15 angel of light. Therefore it is no great thing if his ministers also be transformed as the ministers of righteousness; 16 whose end shall be according to their works. I say again, Let no man think me a fool; if otherwise, yet as a fool 17 receive me, that I may boast myself a little. That which I speak, I speak it not after the Lord, but as it were 18 foolishly, in this confidence of boasting. Seeing that 19 many glory after the flesh, I will glory also. For ye suffer 20 fools gladly, seeing ye yourselves are wise. For ye suffer, if a man bring you into bondage, if a man devour you, if a man take of you, if a man exalt himself, if a man smite 21 you on the face. I speak as concerning reproach, as though we had been weak. Howbeit whereinsoever any 22 is bold, (I speak foolishly,) I am bold also. Are they Hebrews? so am I. Are they Israelites? so am I. Are 23 they the seed of Abraham? so am I. Are they ministers

of Christ? (I speak as a fool) I am more; in labours more abundant, in stripes above measure, in prisons more frequent, in deaths oft. Of the Jews five times received I 24 forty stripes save one. Thrice was I beaten with rods, 25 once was I stoned, thrice I suffered shipwreck, a night and a day I have been in the deep; in journeyings often, in 26 perils of waters, in perils of robbers, in perils by mine own countrymen, in perils by the heathen, in perils in the city, in perils in the wilderness, in perils in the sea, in perils among false brethren; in weariness and painfulness, 27 in watchings often, in hunger and thirst, in fastings often, in cold and nakedness. Beside those things that are 28 without, that which cometh upon me daily, the care of all the churches. Who is weak, and I am not weak? who is 29 offended, and I burn not? If I must needs glory, I will 30 glory of the things which concern mine infirmities. The 31 God and Father of our Lord Jesus Christ, which is blessed for evermore, knoweth that I lie not. In Damascus the 32 governor under Aretas the king kept the city of the Damascenes with a garrison, desirous to apprehend me: and 33 through a window in a basket was I let down by the wall, and escaped his hands.

It is not expedient for me doubtless to glory. I will **12** come to visions and revelations of the Lord. I knew a 2 man in Christ above fourteen years ago, (whether in the body, I cannot tell; or whether out of the body, I cannot tell: God knoweth;) such an one caught up to the third heaven. And I knew such a man, (whether in the body, 3 or out of the body, I cannot tell: God knoweth;) how 4 that he was caught up into paradise, and heard unspeakable words, which it is not lawful for a man to utter. Of such 5 an one will I glory: yet of myself I will not glory, but in mine infirmities. For though I would desire to glory, I 6

shall not be a fool; for I will say the truth: but now I forbear, lest any man should think of me above that which
7 he seeth me to be, or that he heareth of me. And lest I should be exalted above measure through the abundance of the revelations, there was given to me a thorn in the flesh, the messenger of Satan to buffet me, lest I should
8 be exalted above measure. For this thing I besought the
9 Lord thrice, that it might depart from me. And he said unto me, My grace is sufficient for thee: for my strength is made perfect in weakness. Most gladly therefore will I rather glory in my infirmities, that the power of Christ may
10 rest upon me. Therefore I take pleasure in infirmities, in reproaches, in necessities, in persecutions, in distresses for
11 Christ's sake: for when I am weak, then am I strong. I am become a fool in glorying: ye have compelled me: for I ought to have been commended of you: for in nothing am I behind the very chiefest apostles, though I be nothing.
12 Truly the signs of an apostle were wrought among you in all patience, in signs, and wonders, and mighty deeds.
13 For what is it wherein ye were inferior to other churches, except it be that I myself was not burdensome to you?
14 forgive me this wrong. Behold, I am ready to come to you this third time; and I will not be burdensome to you: for I seek not your's, but you: for the children ought not to lay up for the parents, but the parents for the children.
15 And I will very gladly spend and be spent for you; though
16 the more abundantly I love you, the less I be loved. But be it so, I did not burden you: nevertheless, being crafty,
17 I caught you with guile. Did I make a gain of you by
18 any of them whom I sent unto you? I desired Titus, and with him I sent a brother. Did Titus make a gain of you? walked we not in the same spirit? walked we not in the
19 same steps? All this time ye think that we are excusing

II. CORINTHIANS

ourselves unto you? we speak before God in Christ: but we do all things, dearly beloved, for your edifying. For I fear, 20 lest, when I come, I shall not find you such as I would, and that I shall be found unto you such as ye would not: lest there be debates, envyings, wraths, strifes, backbitings, whisperings, swellings, tumults: and lest, when I come 21 again, my God will humble me among you, and that I shall bewail many which have sinned already, and have not repented of the uncleanness and fornication and lasciviousness which they have committed.

This third time I am coming to you. At the mouth 13 of two witnesses and three shall every word be established. I have warned, and I warn, as when I was present the 2 second time, so also when I am absent now, those that have sinned before, and all the rest, that, if I come again, I will not spare: since ye seek a proof of Christ 3 speaking in me, which to you-ward is not weak, but is mighty in you. For though he was crucified through 4 weakness, yet he liveth by the power of God. For we also are weak in him, but we shall live with him by the power of God toward you. Examine yourselves, whether 5 ye be in the faith; prove your own selves. Know ye not your own selves, how that Jesus Christ is in you, except ye be reprobates? But I trust that ye shall know that we 6 are not reprobates. Now I pray to God that ye do no 7 evil; not that we should appear approved, but that ye should do that which is honest, though we be as reprobates. For we can do nothing against the truth, but for the truth. 8 For we are glad, when we are weak, and ye are strong: 9 and this also we wish, even your perfection. Therefore 10 I write these things being absent, lest being present I should use sharpness, according to the power which the Lord hath given me to edification, and not to destruction.

II. CORINTHIANS

11 Finally, brethren, farewell. Be perfect, be of good comfort, be of one mind, live in peace; and the God of
12 love and peace shall be with you. Greet one another
13 with an holy kiss. All the saints salute you.
14 The grace of the Lord Jesus Christ, and the love of God, and the communion of the Holy Ghost, be with you all. Amen.

THE THIRD EPISTLE OF PAUL THE APOSTLE TO THE CORINTHIANS

PAUL, an apostle of Jesus Christ by the will of God, and 1
Timothy our brother, unto the church of God which is at
Corinth, with all the saints which are in all Achaia: Grace 2
be to you and peace from God our Father, and from the
Lord Jesus Christ. Blessed be God, even the Father of 3
our Lord Jesus Christ, the Father of mercies, and the God
of all comfort; who comforteth us in all our tribulation, 4
that we may be able to comfort them which are in any
trouble, by the comfort wherewith we ourselves are comforted of God. For as the sufferings of Christ abound in 5
us, so our consolation also aboundeth by Christ. And 6
whether we be afflicted, it is for your consolation and
salvation, which is effectual in the enduring of the same
sufferings which we also suffer: or whether we be comforted,
it is for your consolation and salvation. And our hope of 7
you is stedfast, knowing, that as ye are partakers of the
sufferings, so shall ye be also of the consolation. For we 8
would not, brethren, have you ignorant of our trouble
which came to us in Asia, that we were pressed out of
measure, above strength, insomuch that we despaired even
of life: but we had the sentence of death in ourselves, 9
that we should not trust in ourselves, but in God which
raiseth the dead: who delivered us from so great a death, 10
and doth deliver: in whom we trust that he will yet deliver

11 us; ye also helping together by prayer for us, that for the gift bestowed upon us by the means of many persons thanks may be given by many on our behalf.

12 For this boasting of ours is the testimony of our conscience, that in simplicity and godly sincerity, not with fleshly wisdom, but by the grace of God, we have had our conversation in the world, and more abundantly to you-
13 ward. For we write none other things than those which ye acknowledge, or even maintain, and I hope that ye will
14 maintain even to the end, as in part even *in the past* ye maintained of us that we are your boast, as also ye are ours
15 in the day of our Lord Jesus. And in this confidence I was wishing to come before unto you that ye might have a
16 second benefit; both to pass through you to Macedonia, and again from Macedonia to come to you, and by you
17 to be sent on to Judæa. Was I thoughtless when I was cherishing this wish? or the things that I resolve do I resolve according to the flesh, that with me there should be the yea
18 yea, and the nay nay? But as God is true, our word toward
19 you was not yea and nay. For the Son of God, Jesus Christ, who was preached among you by us, even by me and Silvanus and Timotheus, was not yea and nay, but in
20 him was yea. For all the promises of God in him are yea,
21 and in him Amen, unto the glory of God by us. Now he which stablisheth us with you in Christ, and hath anointed
22 us, is God; who hath also sealed us, and given the earnest
23 of the Spirit in our hearts. But I call God for a witness upon my soul, that to spare you I came no more unto
24 Corinth. Not for that we have dominion over your faith, but are helpers of your joy: for by faith ye stand.

2 But I determined this with myself, that I would not
2 come again to you with sorrow. For if I make you sorry, who is he then that maketh me glad, but the same which

III. CORINTHIANS

is made sorry by me? And I wrote this same unto you, 3
lest, when I came, I should have sorrow from them of
whom I ought to rejoice; having confidence in you all, that
my joy is the joy of you all. For out of much affliction 4
and anguish of heart I wrote unto you with many tears;
not that ye should be grieved, but that ye might know
the love which I have more abundantly unto you. But if 5
any have caused grief, he hath not grieved me, but in part:
that I may not overcharge you all. Sufficient to such a 6
man is this punishment, which was inflicted by the majority.
So that on the contrary it is for you rather to forgive 7
him and comfort him, lest perhaps such a one should be
swallowed up with overmuch sorrow. Wherefore I beseech 8
you that ye would confirm your love toward him. For to 9
this end also did I write, that I might know the proof of
you, whether ye be obedient in all things. To whom ye 10
forgive any thing, I forgive also: for if I forgave any thing,
to whom I forgave it, for your sakes forgave I it in the
person of Christ; lest Satan should get an advantage of 11
us: for we are not ignorant of his devices. Furthermore, 12
when I came to Troas to preach Christ's gospel, and a
door was opened unto me of the Lord, I had no rest in 13
my spirit, because I found not Titus my brother: but
taking my leave of them, I went from thence into Macedonia. Now thanks be unto God, which always causeth us 14
to triumph in Christ, and maketh manifest the savour of
his knowledge by us in every place. For we are unto God 15
a sweet savour of Christ, in them that are saved, and in
them that perish: to the one we are the savour of death 16
unto death; and to the other the savour of life unto life.
And who is sufficient for these things? For we are not as 17
many, which corrupt the word of God: but as of sincerity,
but as of God, in the sight of God speak we in Christ.

3 Do we begin again to commend ourselves? or need we, as some others, epistles of commendation to you, or letters
2 of commendation from you? Ye are our epistle written in
3 our hearts, known and acknowledged by all men; being made manifest that ye are an epistle of Christ ministered by us, written not with ink, but with the Spirit of the living God; not in tables of stone, but in fleshy tables of
4 the heart. And such trust have we through Christ to
5 God-ward: not that we are sufficient of ourselves to think any thing as of ourselves; but our sufficiency is of God;
6 who also hath made us able ministers of the new testament; not of the letter, but of the spirit: for the letter killeth,
7 but the spirit giveth life. But if the ministration of death, written and engraven in stones, was glorious, so that the children of Israel could not stedfastly behold the face of Moses for the glory of his countenance; which glory was
8 to be done away: how shall not the ministration of
9 the spirit be rather glorious? For if the ministration of condemnation be glory, much more doth the ministration
10 of righteousness exceed in glory. For even that which was made glorious had no glory in this respect, by reason of
11 the glory that excelleth. For if that which is done away was glorious, much more that which remaineth is glorious.
12 Seeing then that we have such hope, we use great plainness
13 of speech: and not as Moses, which put a vail over his face, that the children of Israel could not stedfastly look
14 to the end of that which was passing away: but their minds were blinded: for until this day remaineth the same vail untaken away in the reading of the old testament; which
15 vail is done away in Christ. But even unto this day, when
16 Moses is read, the vail is upon their heart. Nevertheless when it shall turn to the Lord, the vail shall be taken away.
17 Now the Lord is that Spirit: and where the Spirit of the

Lord is, there is liberty. But we all, with open face 18 beholding as in a mirror the glory of the Lord, are changed into the same image from glory to glory, even as by the Lord the Spirit.

Therefore seeing we have this ministry, as we have 4 received mercy, we faint not; but have renounced the 2 hidden things of dishonesty, not walking in craftiness, nor handling the word of God deceitfully; but by manifestation of the truth commending ourselves to every man's conscience in the sight of God. But if our gospel be hid, it is hid to 3 them that are lost: in whom the god of this world hath 4 blinded the minds of them which believe not, lest the light of the glorious gospel of Christ, who is the image of God, should shine unto them. For we preach not 5 ourselves, but Christ Jesus the Lord; and ourselves your servants for Jesus' sake. For God, who commanded the 6 light to shine out of darkness, hath shined in our hearts, to give the light of the knowledge of the glory of God in the face of Jesus Christ. But we have this treasure in earthen 7 vessels, that the excellency of the power may be of God, and not of us. We are troubled on every side, yet not 8 distressed; we are perplexed, but not in despair; persecuted, 9 but not forsaken; cast down, but not destroyed; always 10 bearing about in the body the dying of the Lord Jesus, that the life also of Jesus might be made manifest in our body. For we which live are alway delivered unto death 11 for Jesus' sake, that the life also of Jesus might be made manifest in our mortal flesh. So then death worketh in us, 12 but life in you. We having the same spirit of faith, accord- 13 ing as it is written, I believed, and therefore have I spoken; we also believe, and therefore speak; knowing that he 14 which raised up the Lord Jesus shall raise up us also by Jesus, and shall present us with you. For all things are 15

for your sakes, that the abundant grace might through the
16 thanksgiving of many redound to the glory of God. For
which cause we faint not; but though our outward man
17 perish, yet the inward man is renewed day by day. For
our light affliction, which is but for a moment, worketh for
18 us a far more exceeding and eternal weight of glory; while
we look not at the things which are seen, but at the things
which are not seen: for the things which are seen are
temporal; but the things which are not seen are eternal.

5 For we know that if our earthly house of this tabernacle
were dissolved, we have a building of God, an house not
2 made with hands, eternal in the heavens. For in this we
groan, earnestly desiring to be clothed upon with our house
3 which is from heaven: if so be that being clothed we shall
4 not be found naked. For we that are in this tabernacle
do groan, being burdened: not for that we would be
unclothed, but clothed upon, that mortality might be
5 swallowed up of life. Now he that hath wrought us for
the selfsame thing is God, who also hath given unto us the
6 earnest of the Spirit. Therefore we are always confident,
knowing that, whilst we are at home in the body, we are
7 absent from the Lord: (for we walk by faith, not by sight:)
8 we are confident, I say, and willing rather to be absent from
9 the body, and to be present with the Lord. Wherefore we
labour, that, whether present or absent, we may be accepted
10 of him. For we must all appear before the judgment seat
of Christ; that every one may receive the things done in
his body, according to that he hath done, whether it be
11 good or bad. Knowing therefore the terror of the Lord,
we persuade men; but we are made manifest unto God;
and I trust also are made manifest in your consciences.
12 For we commend not ourselves again unto you, but give
you occasion to glory on our behalf, that ye may have

III. CORINTHIANS

somewhat to answer them which glory in appearance, and
not in heart. For whether we be beside ourselves, it is to 13
God: or whether we be sober, it is for your cause. For 14
the love of Christ constraineth us; because we thus judge,
that if one died for all, then were all dead: and that he 15
died for all, that they which live should not henceforth live
unto themselves, but unto him which died for them, and
rose again. Wherefore henceforth know we no man after 16
the flesh: yea, though we have known Christ after the
flesh, yet now henceforth know we him no more. There- 17
fore if any man be in Christ, he is a new creature: old
things are passed away; behold, all things are become new.
And all things are of God, who hath reconciled us to him- 18
self by Jesus Christ, and hath given to us the ministry of
reconciliation; to wit, that God was in Christ, reconciling 19
the world unto himself, not imputing their trespasses unto
them; and hath committed unto us the word of reconciliation. Now then we are ambassadors for Christ, as though 20
God did beseech you by us: we pray you in Christ's stead,
be ye reconciled to God. For he hath made him to be sin 21
for us, who knew no sin; that we might be made the
righteousness of God in him.

We then, as workers together with him, beseech you also **6**
that ye receive not the grace of God in vain. (For he 2
saith, I have heard thee in a time accepted, and in the day
of salvation have I succoured thee: behold, now is the
accepted time; behold, now is the day of salvation.)
Giving no offence in any thing, that the ministry be not 3
blamed: but in all things approving ourselves as the 4
ministers of God, in much patience, in afflictions, in
necessities, in distresses, in stripes, in imprisonments, in 5
tumults, in labours, in watchings, in fastings; by pureness, 6
by knowledge, by longsuffering, by kindness, by the Holy

7 Ghost, by love unfeigned, by the word of truth, by the power of God, by the armour of righteousness on the right 8 hand and on the left, by honour and dishonour, by evil 9 report and good report: as deceivers, and yet true; as unknown, and yet well known; as dying, and, behold, we 10 live; as chastened, and not killed; as sorrowful, yet alway rejoicing; as poor, yet making many rich; as having 11 nothing, and yet possessing all things. O ye Corinthians, 12 our mouth is open unto you, our heart is enlarged. Ye are not straitened in us, but ye are straitened in your own 13 bowels. Now for a recompence in the same, (I speak 14 as unto my children,) be ye also enlarged. Be ye not unequally yoked together with unbelievers: for what fellowship hath righteousness with unrighteousness? and what 15 communion hath light with darkness? And what concord hath Christ with Belial? or what part hath he that believeth 16 with an infidel? And what agreement hath the temple of God with idols? for ye are the temple of the living God; as God hath said, I will dwell in them, and walk in them; and I will be their God, and they shall be my people. 17 Wherefore come out from among them, and be ye separate, saith the Lord, and touch not the unclean thing; and 18 I will receive you, and will be a Father unto you, and ye shall be my sons and daughters, saith the Lord Almighty.

7 Having therefore these promises, dearly beloved, let us cleanse ourselves from all filthiness of the flesh and spirit, 2 perfecting holiness in the fear of God. Receive us; we have wronged no man, we have corrupted no man, we have 3 defrauded no man. I speak not this to condemn you: for I have said before, that ye are in our hearts to die and live 4 with you. Great is my boldness of speech toward you, great is my glorying of you: I am filled with comfort, I am 5 exceeding joyful in all our tribulation. For, when we were

III. CORINTHIANS

come into Macedonia, our flesh had no rest, but we were troubled on every side; without were fightings, within were fears. Nevertheless God, that comforteth those that are 6 cast down, comforted us by the coming of Titus; and not 7 by his coming only, but by the consolation wherewith he was comforted in you, when he told us your earnest desire, your mourning, your fervent mind toward me; so that I rejoiced the more. For though I made you sorry 8 with a letter, I do not repent, though I did repent: for I perceive that the same epistle hath made you sorry, though it were but for a season. Now I rejoice, not 9 that ye were made sorry, but that ye sorrowed to repentance: for ye were made sorry after a godly manner, that ye might receive damage by us in nothing. For godly sorrow 10 worketh repentance to salvation not to be repented of: but the sorrow of the world worketh death. For behold 11 this selfsame thing, that ye sorrowed after a godly sort, what carefulness it wrought in you, yea, what clearing of yourselves, yea, what indignation, yea, what fear, yea, what vehement desire, yea, what zeal, yea, what revenge! In all things ye have approved yourselves to be clear in this matter. Wherefore, though I wrote unto you, I did it 12 not for his cause that had done the wrong, nor for his cause that suffered wrong, but that our care for you in the sight of God might appear unto you. Therefore we were 13 comforted in your comfort: yea, and exceedingly the more joyed we for the joy of Titus, because his spirit was refreshed by you all. For if I have boasted any thing 14 to him of you, I am not ashamed; but as we spake all things to you in truth, even so our boasting, which I made before Titus, is found a truth. And his inward affection is 15 more abundant toward you, whilst he remembereth the obedience of you all, how with fear and trembling ye

16 received him. I rejoice therefore that I have confidence in you in all things.

8 Moreover, brethren, we do you to wit of the grace of 2 God bestowed on the churches of Macedonia; how that in a great trial of affliction the abundance of their joy and their deep poverty abounded unto the riches of their 3 liberality. For to their power, I bear record, yea, and 4 beyond their power they were willing of themselves; praying us with much intreaty that we would receive the gift, and take upon us the fellowship of the ministering to the 5 saints. And this they did, not as we hoped, but first gave their own selves to the Lord, and unto us by the will of 6 God. Insomuch that we called on Titus in order that as he had made a beginning, so he would accomplish this grace 7 also in you: yea, that, as ye abound in everything, in faith, and utterance, and knowledge, and in all earnestness, and in 8 your love to us, so ye may abound in this grace also. I speak not by commandment, but by occasion of the forwardness 9 of others, and to prove the sincerity of your love. For ye know the grace of our Lord Jesus Christ, that, though he was rich, yet for your sakes he became poor, that ye 10 through his poverty might be rich. And herein I give my advice: for this is expedient for you, who have begun before, not only to do, but also to be forward a year ago. 11 Now therefore perform the doing of it; that as there was a readiness to will, so there may be a performance also out 12 of that which ye have. For if there be first a willing mind, it is accepted according to that a man hath, and not 13 according to that he hath not. For I mean not that other 14 men be eased, and ye burdened: but by an equality, that now at this time your abundance may be a supply for their want, that their abundance also may be a supply for your 15 want: that there may be equality: as it is written, He that had gathered much had nothing over; and he that had gathered little had no lack. But thanks be to God, which 16 put the same earnest care into the heart of Titus for you. For indeed he accepted the exhortation; but being more 17 forward, of his own accord he went unto you. And we 18 have sent with him the brother, whose praise is in the gospel throughout all the churches; and not that only, but 19 who was also chosen of the churches to travel with us with this grace, which is administered by us to the glory of the same Lord, and declaration of your ready mind: avoiding 20 this, that no man should blame us in this abundance which is administered by us: providing for honest things, not 21 only in the sight of the Lord, but also in the sight of men. And we have sent with them our brother, whom we have 22 oftentimes proved diligent in many things, but now much more diligent, upon the great confidence which I have in you. Whether any do enquire of Titus, he is my partner 23 and fellowhelper concerning you: or our brethren be enquired of, they are the messengers of the churches, and the glory of Christ. Wherefore shew ye to them, and before 24 the churches, the proof of your love, and of our boasting on your behalf.

For as touching the ministering to the saints, it is super- 9 fluous for me to write to you: for I know the forwardness 2 of your mind, for which I boast of you to them of Macedonia, that Achaia was ready a year ago; and your zeal hath provoked very many. Yet have I sent the 3 brethren, lest our boasting of you should be in vain in this behalf; that, as I said, ye may be ready: lest haply if they 4 of Macedonia come with me, and find you unprepared, we (that we say not, ye) should be ashamed in this same confident boasting. Therefore I thought it necessary to 5 exhort the brethren, that they would go before unto you, and make up beforehand your bounty, whereof ye had notice before, that the same might be ready, as a matter 6 of bounty, and not as of covetousness. But this I say, He which soweth sparingly shall reap also sparingly; and he 7 which soweth bountifully shall reap also bountifully. Every man according as he purposeth in his heart, so let him give; not grudgingly, or of necessity: for God loveth a 8 cheerful giver. And God is able to make all grace abound toward you; that ye, always having all sufficiency in all 9 things, may abound to every good work: (as it is written, He hath dispersed abroad; he hath given to the poor: his 10 righteousness remaineth for ever. Now he that ministereth seed to the sower both minister bread for your food, and multiply your seed sown, and increase the fruits of your 11 righteousness;) being enriched in every thing to all bountifulness, which causeth through us thanksgiving to God. 12 For the administration of this service not only supplieth the want of the saints, but is abundant also by many 13 thanksgivings unto God; whiles by the experiment of this ministration they glorify God for your professed subjection unto the gospel of Christ, and for your liberal distribution 14 unto them, and unto all men; and by their prayer for you, which long after you for the exceeding grace of God in you.

15   Thanks be unto God for his unspeakable gift.